Trevor Bailey

TREVOR BAILEY

A Life in Cricket

JACK BAILEY

Methuen

First published in Great Britain in 1993
by Methuen,
Michelin House, 81 Fulham Road, London SW3 6RB

Copyright © 1993 Jack Bailey

A CIP catalogue record for this book
is available from the British Library
ISBN 0 413 662403

Photoset by Deltatype Ltd, Ellesmere Port, Cheshire
Printed in Great Britain
by Clays Ltd, St. Ives plc

Contents

Acknowledgements   vii

Foreword by Keith Miller   ix

Prologue   1

1 The Making of a Cricketer 1931–48   9

2 On his way to the Top 1948–52   27

3 At the Height of his Powers 1953   50

4 Vice-captain to Hutton 1953–54   74

5 England and Essex and a Winter in Australia 1954–55   93

6 The Middle Years 1955–58   113

7 The Last Tests 1958–59   131

8 Elder Statesman 1959–67   140

Epilogue   157

Appendix 1: Batting and Bowling Statistics   169

Appendix 2: Four scorecards   174

Index   179

Acknowledgements

A biography should be an accurate portrayal of the subject, so far as that is ever possible. Thus objectivity should be the biographer's watchword. It is a difficult process, and it is made the more difficult, the better you know the subject. I can only hope that Trevor Bailey's many friends and acquaintances will recognise the real Trevor somewhere in this book. I hope, too, that something like justice has been done to him, both as a cricketer and a man of real worth.

Thanks are due to many. Among them are those who, however unwittingly, in the course of the past twenty-five years or so have passed on the odd anecdote about Trevor Bailey to add to my own experience of him. More specifically, my thanks go to the following for permission to quote from publications which refer to Trevor Bailey: Heinemann & Co. for *Cricket from the Middle* by D. J. Insole, 1960; Constable & Co. for *Australia '55* by Alan Ross, 1955; Stanley Paul for *Fifty Years in Cricket* by Sir Leonard Hutton and Alex Bannister, 1984; Grafton/Collins for *Gentlemen and Players* by Michael Marshall, 1987; the Kingswood Press for *Essex County Cricket Club: the Complete History* by David Lemmon and Mike Marshall, 1987. In addition, a select bibliography must include: *Wisden Cricketers' Almanack*, 1939–1992; *Barclays World of Cricket; Cricket Heroes* (Headline Publications); *Wickets, Catches and the Odd Run*, by T. E. Bailey (Collins/Willow); and issues of *The Times* between 1946–1993.

I must also thank the Hulton-Deutsch Collection for their kind permission to reproduce the photographs numbered 4, 5, 8, 9 and 14; and the S & G Press Agency for their kind permission to reproduce nos. 6, 7, 10, 11, 13 and 16.

Certainly not least, though almost last, I owe a debt of gratitude to Keith Miller, Trevor's old foe, for agreeing to write the foreword. He has clearly lost none of his generosity of spirit. My thanks, too, to my wife, Vivian, for her unstinting help with the manuscript and, of course, to Tony Pocock, my editor, who, in his quiet, unfailing way, has been a great source of strength.

Finally, to Trevor and Greta Bailey, my grateful thanks for their kindness, their help, their co-operation and their hospitality.

London 1993   Jack Bailey

Foreword

I find myself immensely pleased to have been asked to contribute to a book about Trevor Bailey. There have been occasions during the past forty years or so when, I must admit, I would have doubted whether this would be so. Trevor was so often such a pain if you were playing for Australia against him – a damned nuisance in fact. You knew that if you could get this bloke out of the way, the chances were you would win. All too often he played a large part in denying us. All too frequently Ray Lindwall and I would find it a task beyond us, and that got under our skin.

Another reason I was so pleased to write this foreword is because I'm not at all sure that Trevor's part in England's success during some very tough games against Australia has been recognised as it should have been. More than just the runs he scored or the wickets he took was his ability to stiffen the resolve of any side he played for. He was a fighter, and for all the frustration and annoyance he often caused us, we admired him for that, above all.

We did not of course show much admiration on the field, nor would he have expected it. But we could not help but appreciate, as cricketers, his guts, his technical skill and his wide knowledge of the game. He employed these assets in a way the toughest Australian could understand even if not always approve: Lord's and Leeds in 1953 were supreme examples.

I have lost count of the times I found myself cursing Trevor's ability to make life awkward for me and my fellow Australians. But Trevor and I have always been good friends, even though he never paid me back for that wicket I gave him at Southend in 1948. Another old mate of mine, Jack Bailey, has written a book about him which I know will be enjoyed. It is, I think, true to the essential Trevor Bailey, and I commend it to you.

Newport Beach,
New South Wales
1993
                                          Keith Miller

Prologue

Writing of his days at Dulwich College, where his record as a schoolboy cricketer was one of unparalleled success, from his first appearance at the age of fourteen to his last, Trevor Bailey makes an interesting statement. 'In my last year at Dulwich,' he says, 'although I did not make as many runs as in 1941, I had my best all-round summer, scoring 635 runs and capturing 66 wickets at 6.17, which was necessary as Kiddle was then in the RAF.' Horace Kiddle was a fast bowler of great promise. He had taken more than 50 wickets during the previous season and, had he not been killed flying in the war, would almost certainly have played for Surrey. But the point of quoting that sentence of Trevor's lies in the use of the word 'necessary'. It was 'necessary', so he took 66 wickets. In a way it sums up his life.

In his excellent book, *Fred – Portrait of a Fast Bowler*, John Arlott says: 'There is not one Fred Trueman but four – the basic Fred Trueman, Fred Trueman the fast bowler, Fred Trueman the man, and Fred Trueman the public image.' Later, he says, 'No one knows Fred Trueman completely: and none of those who know Fred Trueman at all would agree about him – if only for the fact that no two of them have seen the same Fred Trueman.' By the same criteria it would be difficult to find two people who disagree about Trevor Bailey in the essentials.

As someone who has gone through life doing what was 'necessary', often by doing what came naturally, he has presented a constant, straightforward, easily labelled, quickly identifiable face to the world. None of which is to say that he is anything but a complicated, sensitive human being, or any less complex than the most artistic soul.

1

It is just that he has assessed his limits and his limitations, has early seen his role in life, and has played that role quite marvellously well.

By doing what has been 'necessary' Trevor has been able to live up to standards higher than many would dream of attaining. He had great gifts as an athlete and a player of ball games which interested him; he had the wonderful asset of being able to gauge the right course of action for him, given a certain set of circumstances; and above all, perhaps, he had the ability to function to requirements as 'necessary'. He has had his disappointments, and many of them, but his ratio of success to failure – on the cricket field, the soccer field, and the broader pastures of life itself – has been high.

Whether the role he saw for himself, and played to the hilt, has been entirely worthy of his talents remains open to some small debate; but only among the least generous critics of the game. He has done what he felt was necessary in every given situation, and he has succeeded. If there have been times when his vision seemed not a little limited, well, he would be the last to assert that he was perfect in any aspect of his life. But, by and large, he can claim to have remained true to his ideals and to himself. Know one Trevor Bailey and you know them all.

Doing the 'necessary' has meant life in a number of varied activities. The seven ages of man has nothing on Trevor Bailey. While he was playing cricket for Essex and England he was at the same time playing top-class amateur association football, writing articles, serving as assistant secretary of Essex County Cricket Club, helping to found an indoor cricket school; he was a director of Southend United FC, and was engaged in various promotional and business activities. While all this was going on, he was, at various times, a thorn in the flesh of his opponents on the field; predictable in his stubborn defiance, unpredictable only in his many shafts of brilliance.

In his life, he went doggedly in pursuit of what he felt was necessary for a good, enjoyable life for his family and himself. By no means avaricious beyond the dreams of man, he went for what he considered rightfully his; for what he was worth: no more, and certainly no less. As

2

a result, he has carved a way which has brought a long and lasting marriage; three children, all given the best in education; and a lasting place in the folklore of cricket.

If you had to condense his career – and his demeanour – into a paragraph, rather than having the pleasure of writing a book about him, you could do a lot worse than borrow from John Woodcock of *The Times* writing about Trevor in the 1969 *Wisden* a couple of years after Bailey had finally consigned his first-class cricket boots to a place of rest:

'The custom of topping 100 wickets in a season and passing 1,000 runs began in 1949. Eight times he achieved it, and in 1959 he scored 2,011 runs, besides collecting 100 wickets. Once against Lancashire at Clacton in 1949, he took all ten wickets in an innings. All told he made 28,642 runs and took 2,082 wickets. Nine times he headed the Essex bowling averages, seven times the batting. He was their secretary from 1954 until 1965, and their captain from 1961 until 1966. To the young cricketers of Essex he was guide, philosopher and friend. To the powers-that-be he tended to seem too cynical. He was kind yet intolerant, thoughtful yet outspoken, cautious yet successful, precise yet amusing, aloof yet companionable. If you had asked the county players of the 1960s who was the best first-class captain, they would have replied, almost to a man, 'Give me Trevor'. It was his shrewdness they respected, as well, of course, as his record.'

With one or two slight changes of direction as a result of conscious decisions taken along the way, Bailey's life seems to have been mapped out from his very early days. His natural talents for all form of ball games soon surfaced. His independent streak quickly showed, first when he virtually taught himself to play cricket; then when, as a prep-school boy at Alleyn Court, he stuck to being an all-rounder – fast bowler and dashing batsman – rather than continue with batting as his main last, and this against the advice of his guide, mentor and headmaster, Denys Wilcox.

3

Bailey was right about that. He was too talented a bowler, too anxious to be part of every facet of the game, too certain of his ability to work out the weaknesses of an opponent to have been able to sit back and watch things going wrong around him. Besides, he came to realise that batting and bowling gave him two chances to one of success – and personal success was an important part of his make-up. Three wickets and 50 runs as an all-rounder earned him marks as high as a century as a batsman. Anything else was a bonus; anything less could still mark a creditable performance. And he could field and catch with the best of them.

This book is chiefly about cricket. For it is as a cricketer that Bailey is famous, and the cricket field was the scene of his greatest exploits. But he was a player of association football good enough to gain a Blue at Cambridge – although he played only rugby football at Dulwich – and to go on to play with distinction in an Amateur Cup final won by his side, Walthamstow Avenue; good enough to have been a professional footballer, if he had wanted to, which he did not. There is no doubt that if he had made the time he could have added a squash Blue to his achievements at university. He was a fine athlete at Dulwich, where he was Victor Ludorum.

Cricket became his vehicle because not only did he excel at it, but it was a game of comparative longevity and, in those days, one in which his place in the social structure could be preserved and enhanced. As an amateur cricketer but one who was earning his living from the game, he was seen as an outstanding soldier and automatic officer material. He was able to devote a large part of his life to something at which he excelled and yet be in a position not to be thrown on the scrap heap when it was all over. Less brave souls, with less faith in their ability and in their fitness, might still, even with the gifts possessed by Trevor, have opted for the steady job, playing cricket when they could within the framework of a life in one of the professions – something he himself very nearly chose to do, as a schoolmaster. Instead, he became a cricketer: full-time, though not professional, but at the same time arguably the most 'professional' amateur there has been. No 'jazz-hat' he, but a thorough-going, dedicated, shrewd and gifted performer.

He chose, because it seemed 'necessary', to establish himself as time went by as a resolute batsman with outstanding defensive qualities. Then he became type-cast and went on playing his part – immaculately, successfully, never feeling the need to play Hamlet when he could play two other important roles in the same play. He became renowned for his resolution in the face of great odds and for being a saviour of lost causes. He was all of that, but he was also the basis for many a victory in improbable circumstances, a fact often less well remembered.

He moved up and down the batting order like a yo-yo. Len Hutton began the mode, adopted later by other captains, of using his defensive attributes in the guise of opening batsman in Test matches. He did all that could be asked of him and more. But it was in his more usual position of fourth wicket down that he made his mark, never more indelibly than when he partnered Willie Watson in the match-saving stand at Lord's in 1953 against the Australians, which truly began a trail of defiance against all types of bowling in all sorts of countries, all over the world.

As a bowler, he began fast, but developed gradually into a sharp fast-medium, capable of swing and movement off the seam as well as supreme accuracy. He concentrated always: he knew his lines, and he delivered them unerringly well. After his debut for England in 1949 against New Zealand he was in the England team, virtually without interruption, for a decade. Sometimes he shared the new ball – with Bedser, with Trueman, with Statham, with Tyson. More often, however, he was brought on as first change, coming on to exploit whatever was in the wicket, to probe and to think out the batsman if there was nothing in the pitch.

Some mention has already been made of his record, and there is more to follow. Statistics can only ever be the roughest of guides to a cricketer's true worth but, in Bailey's case, it is relevant to note from the outset that when his Test career ended he had become only the second Englishman to score more than 2,000 runs and take more than 100 wickets in Test matches. (Ironically, in the following season, he scored over 2,000 runs and took over 100 wickets in the county game without finding favour with the selectors.) In days when Test matches and tours were considerably less frequent than they are now, this was an achievement by which to measure an outstanding playing career. He took 6 wickets for 118 in the first innings of his first Test match and scored 93 runs in his second; and he never looked back. What is more, he was of a generation that believed with Walter Hagen in 'taking time to smell the flowers along the way', and he smelled his fair share, though certainly no more.

Before leaving this net and making our way to the middle, it may be as well to examine the equipment and the conditions. When Bailey was in his prime, the bowling was just as fast as now, and the bouncers flew. The bowlers, judged for the no-ball on the rear foot, not the front as today, often dragged that foot and bowled from a place nearer the batsmen. Some fast bowlers got away with throwing without restraint. The pitches were open to the weather, producing a wide range of conditions.

The batsman was called upon for a technique to deal with a number of factors which are not there today. The bowling seldom lacked the full panoply. You had to play the leg-spinner and googly bowler as well as the orthodox spinner and the real 'quickie'. Under these conditions, with bats which were wands compared with the railway sleepers in use now, protection for the batsman was minimal – pads, gloves, thigh-pad for the front leg, rarely more. No helmets were worn then – and batsmen enjoyed better vision as a consequence, but there was more obvious danger against the likes of Lindwall, Miller and company.

Bear all this in mind when you picture Bailey's forward defensive stroke, used unfailingly against even the quickest bowling, the head over the line of the ball, the body behind it, the left hand facing the batsman rather than the bowler, the better to drop the ball dead at the feet. Resolution, yes; courage, certainly.

This was from a man who, at the start, was 5ft 11in and weighed less than 10st. He put on a few pounds with the years, but his hands were always too small, his physique never robust.

Turning again to Woodcock and slightly to paraphrase him,

'He was entirely happy when drawing on his extraordinary reserves of concentration to deny opponents victory, or when frustrating, with length and line, a batsman bent upon attack . . . Bailey's long approach to the wicket culminated in a good action, and in his bowling there was plenty of variety in design. Few bowlers have given less away, and not even Alec Bedser bowled better to left-handers than Bailey. As a fielder, too, he could turn a game. He held some marvellous catches close to the wicket, and if I pick out two of them it is only because they were unforgettable. One was at Melbourne in 1950–51, when . . . he threw himself to his left to catch Lindsay Hassett. This was a staggering catch, taken in a sun hat. Yet it was no better than the one he held on the Saturday afternoon of the Lord's Test match in 1956. Neil Harvey, the victim, saw Bailey at leg-slip catch an authentic glance off Trueman, right-handed and with a full dive. That was an electric moment, often recalled by those who were there.

'There was something faintly improbable about Bailey's appearance when he first came on the scene. His hair was almost too curly; his gestures were elaborately histrionic; his run-up seemed unnecessarily long; his approach was fastidiously anatomical. Yet his record spoke for itself.'

His record went on doing just that and has gone on doing so. Exploitation of his gifts has resulted in a full life and a happy one; the opportunity to do something he loved throughout it has been seized with both hands. He is, even now, content with his lot.

He has kept in touch with the game that became such a large part of his life and, in so doing, he has made for himself a life modest enough materially, but rich in adventure and friendships throughout the world. At the drop of a hat, he has served on MCC committees, broadcast through various media or taken up his pen, and he has always been predictably true to what he believes in. He has always tended to be impatient with fools or those he considers to be charlatans. As in cricket, so in later life: not immediately everyone's cup of tea, but confoundedly right more often than not, his place in cricket history is assured.

1

The Making of a Cricketer

1931–48

By the standards of the day, Trevor Edward Bailey was born into a
middle-class family. Father was a middle-rank civil servant at the
Admiralty and he commuted daily from Leigh-on-Sea which, if not
highly fashionable, was safely suburban and had the advantage of the
Fenchurch Street line to London. It also combined the healthy sea air
with proximity to the wastes of muddy flats bordering the Thames
estuary known euphemistically as the beach, as well as a modest
garden. He also had a doting mother and a brother, Basil, eleven years
older. All these things were important elements in the development of
young Trevor as a cricketer.

Leigh-on-Sea lies at the genteel end of rumbustious Southend-
on-Sea, with its fun-fairs, kursaal, fish-and-chip shops and cinemas.
From the 1930s onwards, Southend became a boom town, made so by
East-end day-trippers and holiday-makers. Cheap overseas package
tours have eroded the town's prosperity today, but the arterial road
from London remains choc-a-bloc with nose-to-tail traffic at weekends.
Many of those who sail down the A27 for a breath of ozone will be
unaware of Leigh-on-Sea or its neighbour in the sprawl along the
estuary, Westcliff – the two places which throughout his life have been
home for Trevor. Avenues of detached houses are mixed with less
desirable but wholesome enough residences in Leigh, an area where the
principled, temperant, non-conformist church-goer had established an
early grip by the turn of the century, and signs of their dominance still
exist, even to the extent of Temperance hotels.

It all added up to a self-contained life for young Trevor. At the age of
seven he was sent to Alleyn Court, a local and highly regarded

9

preparatory school but, until then, he often had to fall back on his own company, make his own amusements. He was, in effect, an only child, his only brother more like an uncle due to the eleven-year age-gap.

So many household names in cricket and other sports seem to have spent early years in solitary, self-devised games which later were seen as the first signs of a determination to succeed, as well as of precocious talent: Don Bradman in the country town of Bowral, New South Wales, throwing a golf ball against a cylindrical water tank and hitting it as it rebounded, not with a cricket bat but with a stump, perfected his eye and his co-ordination, played imaginary Test matches, equipped himself, almost unknowingly, for a glorious future; Richie Benaud describes matches played on the back veranda with a tennis ball and a cut-down bat, throwing the ball to rebound, hastily adopting a two-handed grip before the ball came back. There are tales, too, of Henry Cotton developing a 'fade' because his golf swing became, perforce, upright when his lone practice took place in a narrow garage.

Young Trevor developed his own game when his father or his brother were unavailable to be cajoled into playing. It involved hours of bowling a ball so that it came back off the wall between the toilet and the garden shed and, having been bowled properly, would be ready to be hit by a bat now held in two hands. He invented the game when he was three years old. There were also the mud-flats of Westcliff-on-Sea: not as glamorous as the stands of Barbados, but ideal for playing cricket, skirted by bathing tents and watched by amused, indulgent parents. The mud was firm, the sea a long way away at low tide, the beached cockle-fishermen's boats lying between the boy cricketer and the sea. Day after day he would play through the long summer. By the time he went to Alleyn Court he could bowl (fast), bat (slog) and field better than any of his Westcliff contemporaries. He could also look after himself in class. From his mother he had learned the joys of reading and was seldom without a book close at hand.

Then Denys Wilcox came into his life. Wilcox senior, father of Denys, had founded the prep school in Westcliff and named it after Edward Alleyn, the Edwardian actor. Alleyn Court had that, and much more besides, in common with Dulwich College. Both Denys and

10

his father were at Dulwich; Denys's son, John, was later to follow the same path as his father and grandfather – Dulwich (but in John's case Malvern), Cambridge, and then headmaster of Alleyn Court. In 1932, Denys had just become joint headmaster, having played for Cambridge University and Essex for a number of years. He had a passion for the game and he was a fine teacher of small boys. He was a product of the school of muscular Christianity which produced a host of teachers at preparatory and public schools. To men like him, the world was a straightforward place. You conformed and you gave 100 per cent to whatever you did.

Wilcox found no difficulty in getting the full attention of this precocious seven-year-old. He spotted immediately that the boy possessed unusual talent. Like so many uncoached boys, he was adroit at hitting the ball to leg, his bowling was fast and furious. So far, a good eye and an ability well beyond that of his peers had brought success in all forms of knock-about cricket. So successful had Trevor been that he had developed certain unbecoming traits. He was – encouraged by the fact that he was virtually an only child – spoilt, petulant and a bad loser.

Nor was he best pleased when Wilcox took him into the nets and swiftly demonstrated that it was the easiest thing in the world to bowl him out, playing as he did. Infuriating though this was, even more galling was the realisation that, by bowling a good length, Wilcox could take his wicket bowling under-arm. This had never happened before. Quickly, the young Bailey learned the value of playing straight if the ball was straight and of a certain length. Quickly, he worked out that good-length bowling was the most difficult to play, and he applied this to his own bowling with marked success.

Wilcox did more than teach him rudimentary techniques. He instilled in Trevor at an extraordinarily early age the need to analyse the strengths and weaknesses of an opponent and to apply the knowledge ruthlessly. So well did Trevor ally this new-found learning to his enthusiasm and his natural ability that, by the time he was nine, he had earned his 1st XI colours in competition with thirteen-year-olds. A year later he was also in the school football team. By the time he left

11

Alleyn Court to go to Dulwich (where else, with the Wilcox influence brought to bear?) he could play any stroke in the book except the hook. At thirteen, after five years in the XI, he finished his last season at the prep school with a record which is unlikely ever to be beaten. He scored more than 1,100 runs in inter-school matches for an average of 138; and took 52 wickets at 7 apiece.

Denys Wilcox tried to persuade Trevor that his future lay with batting. Fast bowling, Wilcox argued, was not, in the long term, a solid investment for a boy barely above average height, slim of build and with small hands. Batting for long periods took immense concentration and quickly consumed what physical resources he had. Wilcox did not want to see one of the most promising batsmen he had known at that age fall between two stools, as he believed Trevor might well do. Trevor, for once, ignored Wilcox's advice. In his mind was the thought that someone who batted *and* bowled was always in the game. If he failed at any particular time at one, he could succeed at the other. Besides he rather fancied himself as a bowler.

Already, the traits which have run strongly within his character throughout his life were beginning to emerge. He would do things, and do them extremely well if, once he had weighed up the checks and balances, assessed the dubious parts from every angle, the idea seemed a good one to him. He would seldom, however, accept the wisdom of others at face value. And he could be persuasive in his own right.

When, for instance, he had spent a couple of years boarding at Dulwich after leaving Alleyn Court, he set about convincing his parents that it would be a good idea if they were to move from Leigh-on-Sea and live in Dulwich. At the age of fifteen or so, he was plainly the apple of his mother's eye, and there were undoubted advantages for his father working in London. But it was something of a coup on his part for, even though living in Southend during the war was no picnic, a move from Leigh to Dulwich could scarcely be rated in terms of avoiding enemy action. Indeed, the first night of the blitz on London coincided exactly with the arrival of his parents in their new home.

The move suited Trevor for several reasons. Dulwich College in war-time was a place of ersatz food and sleeping in air-raid shelters, and life as a boarder had lost much of its appeal. As a day-boy, which Trevor now became, he had more freedom, better food and the chance to mix more openly with the opposite sex. None of this did anything but good for his bowling, which had improved steadily since his arrival at Dulwich.

The wisdom of his choice, to stick to fast bowling is patently obvious now. Then it was touch and go but, in his first year at Dulwich, he was rewarded for having stuck to his guns. At the age of fourteen, he was selected to play for the 1st XI by the captain, Alan Shirreff (later to play for Cambridge University, Hampshire, Kent, Somerset and Combined Services), and he was selected primarily as a quick bowler.

An early match against MCC in 1938 decided the issue. The school had gone into the match with only three bowlers. Jack Robertson, then on the fringes of the Middlesex XI, but later to become a stalwart for the county and to play for England with distinction, so destroyed the Dulwich attack that Shirreff knew that the policy of playing only three bowlers was a mistaken one. So it was that young Bailey was pressed into service as a fourth though not without misgivings on the part of the master in charge. Bailey took a couple of wickets in his first match. Dulwich were playing Bedford School that day, and he still looks upon his inclusion on the team sheet, pinned on the school notice-board, as the most exciting moment in his cricketing career. Relieved, and happy that he had helped to win the match, it can safely be said that he never looked back.

Shy and withdrawn with his seventeen- and eighteen-year-old colleagues, but in no sense overawed, Bailey kept his place for the rest of that season, performed well in the house matches and went on being considered as a bowler who could bat well – a decidedly nippy bowler with a style involving a double windmill arm action and a long, straight run to the wicket. Although drafted in primarily as a bowler, Bailey finished top of the school batting averages with 403 runs at 50.38. His habit of remaining undefeated, later to become a considerable feature of his batting, was in its infancy, but it was there. In thirteen innings he was five times not out.

That and the next four seasons contained many halcyon days. Bailey

13

and Mallett, the Dulwich fast bowlers, became names as familiar in public school circles during those early years of the war as Hutton and Washbrook or Compton and Edrich were to become later in the international sphere. A. W. H. Mallett joined Bailey in the Dulwich side in 1939 to form an opening attack which was generally far too good for schoolboy opposition. Like Bailey, Mallett was a bowler of brisk pace. He was also a batsman of murderous intent with a penchant for hitting the ball out of the ground. He was to pursue the profession of schoolmaster, eventually becoming headmaster of Diocesan College in Cape Town but, while in England, he played with distinction for Kent both during his time at Oxford and after taking a teaching post at Haileybury.

Trevor was not the most popular of opponents. He was too good for one thing. He also lacked Mallett's bluff, genial exterior: the impression he gave, wrapped up in the game as he was, was one of haughty disdain. It was the wrong impression, but it tended to stick. However that may have been, his performances were rich with promise. In 1940, his second season at Dulwich, he was top of the batting and bowling averages. His best season with the bat was in 1941, when he averaged more than 121 runs per innings.

He was captain of cricket and captain of squash, and it was during this season that he had a brief flirtation with leg-spin bowling. That year Dulwich had a bowling attack which was the envy of other schools up and down the land. Apart from Bailey there was Tony Mallett; apart from Mallett there was Horace Kiddle, one of four of Bailey's friends who were to perish in the war, but now a fast bowler with a high action and skilful variations of pace who in 1941 took more than 50 wickets at under 8 runs apiece. Surveying these riches and suffering from a strained back, Bailey decided to give everything to his batting and to bowl leg-breaks. He found that his hands were too small, his temperament not entirely suited to that sort of bowling. He was far from discouraged by the master in charge of cricket, but decided against none the less.

C. S. Marriott, himself a leg-break bowler for Kent and England, was the force behind the wholehearted enthusiasm for cricket at

Dulwich. 'Father', as he had been called for as long as anyone could remember, was an enthusiast for cricket and cricketers. He and the boys were fortunate in their professional, Bill Brown, the ideal net bowler and a source of calm, unhurried wise advice. The pair had an unusual approach. Whereas masters in charge of cricket and coaches at schools were overwhelmingly and exclusively keen on the team under their charge, one small boy, several years after Trevor's time at Dulwich, had reason to be grateful to them both, and he was at Christ's Hospital. In the nets before the Dulwich match, bowling, I was aware of Father Marriott talking to Len Bates, our coach. 'Have you taught him the George Geary ball yet?' he asked Len. 'Yes, but he needs more practice at it before using it in matches,' said Len. Then Marriott asked me to show him the grip *à la* Geary for the leg-cutter and confirmed that it was right and wished me luck. Now that was appreciated.

When the game started, I began to bowl too short on a wet, slow wicket, I was bowling at the end where Brown was umpiring. 'Pitch it up if you want to get him out', was whispered to me about a very good Dulwich opening batsman. Baffled by receiving advice from the opposition, I nevertheless accepted it and was glad I did. But it was a unique experience.

A side-effect of the time spent in the nets with Father Marriott was to serve Trevor well, throughout his school career and far beyond. It made him an excellent player of leg-spin bowling. Later, when playing for England, especially against the Australians with their full complement of leg-spin and 'bosie' men, his reading of the leg-spinner, googly, top-spinner and flipper from such as Doug Ring and Richie Benaud was immaculate, never more profitably than in the second Test at Lord's in 1953 when he batted against them, on and off, for something like five hours and saved the day for England.

By the time he left Dulwich, he was admired and feared by all opponents and – as is the way of schoolboys – often disliked for his matter-of-fact approach to wreaking havoc with bat and ball against all the schools on the Dulwich College fixture-list. At Christ's Hospital, an apocryphal story circulated for years. It concerned the day in 1942 when Christ's Hospital, largely through the agency of a fine all-rounder called Geoffrey Smith, who later played for Kent, inflicted upon Dulwich their only defeat of the season. Bailey, they said, had ordered the page to be ripped out of the Dulwich score-book. A gross, childish calumny, of course, but aloof giants in whatever sphere are subject to that sort of thing, and the more detached they appear to others, the more are such rumours likely to happen.

That summer of 1942, Bailey's last at Dulwich, was his best as an all-rounder. He scored 635 runs for an average of over 50 and took 66 wickets at 6.17. He had become the talk of the cricket world, insofar as there was one in the middle of the war. That Plum Warner, sitting at Lord's, running MCC and promoting as many war-time matches as he could, had noticed the young lad was apparent when he was selected for several representative matches. Bailey captained the Rest against Lord's Schools, and the experience did him no harm. His team were victorious by an innings, he made 49 and took 4 wickets for 20 runs in the Lord's Schools' first innings.

But the two days just before that brought out a performance which had *Wisden* as enthusiastic as, in those days, it was ever wont to be. The cause was a startling first appearance against a combined team from Kent and Surrey, Bailey having been chosen to play for Middlesex and Essex in a two-day match. It was the 3rd and 4th August 1942, and a Bank Holiday crowd of 22,000 was present. They had watched Gubby Allen bowl a first over which had been played easily on a good batsman's pitch, and now they watched the young fast bowler run in, all 9st 12lb of him, with his double windmill action and high leap before delivery. And they saw him take a wicket with his second ball and finish the over with 3 wickets, two of them clean bowled.

Bailey finished with 4 for 36 in that innings. His first appearance at a level approaching first-class had achieved two major landmarks in his thinking. First, he now knew what he had long suspected: the decision made by his elders and betters not to allow him to stand by to play for Essex when the county had enquired after his availability when he was not yet sixteen, had been a good one. Second, he was a natural performer on the big occasion. There may not have been much 'smell of the grease paint', but his first taste of the 'roar of the crowd' was

16

exciting and stimulating. The blood surged, the adrenalin flowed; he *performed*.

The next couple of years or so saw little of Trevor on the cricket field. He was drafted into the Royal Marines, was commissioned – to his considerable surprise, it seems – saw little of what might be called truly active service but did finish with a knowledge of life which his journey along the way thus far had denied him. The Marines was just the outfit if there were rough edges to be smoothed or chips to be knocked off, and Bailey absorbed his years with them with his sense of humour intact. Two aspects of his war-time service had an especially lasting effect. One was that, while he was serving his time largely in Britain, a number of his close friends from Dulwich were killed in action. The other, when finally he embarked for Europe, with the war drawing to a close, was driving across Holland, Belgium and Germany in a Bren carrier: he visited Belsen, and the full horrors of war were brought home to him.

Otherwise, he had it better than most and a great deal better than many. Before going overseas, he had continued to play a lot of cricket for the British Empire XI. He had first played for this charity fund-raising outfit, containing a number of first-class cricketers, while at Dulwich, and now he seized every opportunity offered by whatever leave was available to continue. Then there was inter-services cricket both for the Marines and for the Navy.

There was association football too. Bailey dropped the rugby football he had played throughout his time at Dulwich and returned to the soccer at which he had been so adept at Alleyn Court. As a boy of thirteen, he had been wary of the oval-ball game, disappointed that it was the winter game at Dulwich. He had never quite come to terms with a game which enabled some relatively unskilful boy to cause him considerable physical discomfort, and he did not enjoy tackling or being tackled. But he must have been pretty good, for he was awarded his 1st XV colours. Indeed, his proficiency at soccer served him well on the rugby field. Nowadays, instep kicking at goal is commonplace. Into the 1950s and beyond, the kick at goal, at all levels, was taken with the toe more often than not. The young Bailey at Dulwich did not endear himself greatly to Grahame Parker, the master in charge of rugby, who besides playing for Cambridge University and England was a renowned goal-kicker. Parker was also a cricket Blue, a genial man with Denis Healey eyebrows and a no-nonsense manner who, in later life, became secretary of Gloucestershire CCC. Anyhow, he did not take kindly to being told by some young whippersnapper that it stood to reason that the use of the instep – certainly by the right-footer – for kicks taken from the left-hand side of the posts or from in front would be more certain in both length and direction than the kick taken straight-on with the toe.

It was against all the teaching of the time, but this did not prevent young Bailey explaining that the more of the foot you actually got on to the ball, the better you could control it. Nor did it much help when Trevor proceeded to demonstrate the fact throughout his time at Dulwich, by kicking goals from all over the place in his own version of the round-the-corner method, to the great benefit of every team he played for. Yet rugby football was not for Bailey. He seized on his time in the Marines to improve his prowess in the other code; and played a lot of football and a lot of cricket before being drafted overseas at the end of the war.

But in much of the cricket, though played with a number of good cricketers, many of whom had played for their county – fellow Essex men such as Ray Smith, Sonny Avery and Harry Crabtree among them – the opposition was not always of the highest calibre. So he bowled well enough, batted well too when the opportunity arose, and even played for what passed for an 'England' team, in one-day matches against West Indies, Australia and the Dominions. But it was all a bit too easy. He was not going through a learning process. He was coasting.

He had been coasting in a more general sense, too, ever since leaving Dulwich and joining the Marines. The war-time life of a lieutenant in the services, in England, did little to stretch him. The blind following of orders for someone of his analytical and questioning mind was not geared to enthuse him. But his time had not been wasted. He emerged a more rounded character, though by no means easy or compliant. He had learned something of the mysteries of girls, had learned to drink a pint of two; had learned that there was a harsh life out there, outside the protected and privileged existence he had known before; and learned that the world contained people who could not read or write and for all his good looks and his undeniably superior, public school image, he had established a real empathy with them. But, the war over, he was keen to become ex-Lieutenant Bailey RM.

Salvation came earlier than expected when he was offered a job at his old prep school by his mentor, Denys Wilcox. This had the dual advantage of giving Trevor the opportunity of entering the profession for which he felt he was most suited, and giving him preferment when it came to demobilisation. Which of these factors was uppermost in his mind when he accepted the poorly-paid job of assistant master at a Westcliff-on-Sea prep school goes unrecorded. But it is certain that he had had enough of the Marines and, like Denys Wilcox, he could always, in those days, count on playing cricket for Essex in the holidays. Indeed, in 1945 and 1946, he began to make his mark for the county as well as playing for the British Empire XI, the Lord's XI, and in such unusual first-class fixtures as the Over-33s v the Under-33s.

In any case, a place at Cambridge had been found for him nine months hence. In those days, few colleges would reject someone of Bailey's all-round talent as a games player, however borderline his academic qualifications, and Trevor's academic status was as good as most non-scholars of the day. It is more than likely, however, that someone like him in this day and age would have found it so difficult to get into Cambridge that his career in cricket could have ended then and there.

As it was, the beginning of 1946 saw him looking forward to starting a two-year course at the university in October, happily ensconced at Alleyn Court where it had all begun, and enamoured of a girl called Greta who was destined to become his wife and lifelong supporter in all he attempted. He was just past his twenty-third birthday. He actually enjoyed teaching during those months at Alleyn Court. Everything was in his favour. You have no problems with keeping discipline if you are renowned for your ability at games at the highest level. It was also an occupation suited to his patient, analytical approach. Furthermore, he

19

was home again, in the borough of Southend, where his roots had been all his life and where he would continue to be most at peace.

So much did he enjoy the time spent between leaving the Marines and going up to Cambridge to read English and history that it was his firm conviction that two good years of cricket and football and a decent degree would see him launched on a worthwhile teaching career, and that that would be the life for him. The opportunity to play some county cricket and be involved in all sport was an attractive proposition. A full-time career in cricket was not then an option to be considered seriously.

Those were the days of the amateur and the professional. Nobody who went to Oxford or Cambridge, and very few from any other university for that matter, contemplated the possibility of becoming a pro. The class system of the time – and nowhere was it more starkly illustrated than in cricket – determined absolutely that playing cricket for a living was a notch down the social scale. Within the game there were constant reminders of the difference: separate changing-rooms, at most Test match grounds certainly; the amateurs joining the committee for lunch while the pros ate elsewhere; initials before the surname for the amateur, after the name for the pro. In those and a myriad other small and subtle ways, the distinction was preserved, nowhere more obviously than when the Gentlemen played the Players.

But these social niceties – or nasties, as they might now be called – were not the only matters apparent in the mind of the man educated through the upper stream of the English educational system. The professional's pay was poor. At the end of his career there might be a tax-free benefit, but there was no guarantee. A life in the sun, doing something you were good at, was fine, especially if a life in the mines or some factory was the alternative. But for someone like Trevor Bailey, turning pro was not an option. Looking at the world in 1946, even with Attlee and co. in power, pre-war thinking dominated. The sands were shifting, but imperceptibly.

So a career in teaching was one obvious answer for the well-educated sportsman. Ken Farnes of Essex and England, one of the great fast bowlers just before the war, but a victim of it, had combined teaching with playing at international level. The Royal Liberty School at Romford had indulged his passion for the game and, following an interview there, Trevor came away with the feeling that a similar niche might well follow for him when he finished his two-year course at Cambridge.

The picture Trevor presented to the cricketing world at this stage in his life is encapsulated briefly by Doug Insole, a lifelong friend and colleague. He and Bailey were freshmen at Cambridge together. Describing his impression of Trevor before they met, gained from what he had read in the press, heard around the Essex club cricket circuit, what he'd seen of him playing representative cricket at Lord's, and conversations held with various people who knew him, Insole says:

'I knew . . . that he had been at Denys Wilcox's prep school at Westcliff, where he had been marked down as a future England player from the age of seven; and that he had gone to Dulwich where, I gathered, he wasn't terribly popular, and where he had played his cricket very hard. I had heard at first hand that he played his first match for Essex Club and Ground at the age of fourteen under the astute captaincy of Brian Castor, who was then secretary of Essex and who struck terror (in the nicest possible way) into the hearts of his subordinates. When asked by his captain what he bowled, Trevor had replied: "fast", and in his first over had bowled a very quick ball which was snicked by a tentative batsman to first slip where Mr Castor dropped it easily. I am told that the flow of language from the bowler was at once an education and a delight to the young professionals in the side.'

Insole also relates how, at this time, Bailey's Dulwich comrade, Tony Mallett, was considered a sounder performer. Many critics had written off Trevor as a 'flash-in-the-pan' cricketer.

Thus the twenty-three-year-old undergraduate: he came to Cambridge in 1946 having played for Essex during the previous August and having scored 318 runs and taken 31 wickets. A cricket Blue was a certainty, but what else? Well, there was soccer, and there was squash but, unlike many, Trevor would not quite be able to say that these were the happiest days of his life. So much of the undergraduate existence seemed immature to an ex-Marine. Climbing into college after a late night out seemed unnecessarily tedious. Most weekends were spent back in Essex, paying court to and making plans with the lovely Greta. Other leisure time was strictly limited. He had opted to take his degree in two years, active service allowing him a year's grace from the normal three, and this meant that the thriving social life could not be for him, even had he possessed the wherewithal to pursue it; which he did not. Then there was the time taken by soccer in the winter, cricket in the summer. The path to a Blue at soccer meant two training-sessions and two games a week. Cricket in the summer, was more or less a full-time occupation. He and Greta had become engaged and intended to marry in 1948. So much to do, so little time . . .

University sport was immensely strong for a number of years after the war. The Oxford and Cambridge cricket teams of the day were almost a match for the counties. At Fenner's, Cambridge were powerful enough to avoid being bowled out twice, on a dream of a batsman's wicket, by anyone. Conversely, Trevor found that he had to work hard for his own wickets at Fenner's and, as a consequence, became a better, more thoughtful, bowler. But this took some time to work properly into the system, and there were still times when his reaction to being hit for a run or two was to bowl faster and more furiously. One such notable occasion was when he ran across Martin Donnelly, the great left-handed New Zealand batsman, during the university match of 1947. Oxford scored 457 runs; Donnelly made 81 that day and seemed to take a dislike to Trevor himself at the same time as showing an immense liking for his bowling (*see* Appendix 2). The second Varsity match in which Bailey played saw Cambridge go down by an innings.

Yet university matches, in those days occasions watched by crowds of some 15,000 or more, were by no means the dire occasions for him that they were later to prove for others who went on to great things. Peter May, for example, never really did himself justice in three encounters with Oxford. Bailey, on the other hand, always at home on the big occasion, helped save his team from Oxford with a stubborn 60 not out in his first Varsity match and scored another half-century in the 1948 encounter, this time of a more stimulating vintage, his 50 coming inside an hour and a half. Even so, when Cambridge subsided to that innings defeat, Trevor had plenty of time to prepare himself for his wedding to Greta on the following day.

He had had much on his mind during that summer of 1948, and it was not for him a season to remember with affection. There were finals to be taken, marriage to be contemplated, and a number of injuries which he played through, but which counted against him. Having suffered badly at Cambridge at the hands of the 1948 Australians when not fully fit, he also took the field against them for Essex at Southend and, if anything, suffered even worse. He hitched a lift from Cambridge in mid-term down the arterial road in the Australian coach, an education in itself and quite unlike any other ride he had ever taken in his young life. As all the world knows, the following day saw Essex taken for a ride to the tune of 721 runs in the day. Trevor's share was 2 wickets for more than 120 runs, one of the wickets having been donated by Keith Miller, who is alleged to have been variously either averse 'to taking candy from kids', in the middle of a row with his captain, Don Bradman, or anxious to get back to the pavilion because he had a good hand at poker. I have asked Keith, but he would never divulge the reason why he decided deliberately to miss the first ball he received from Trevor. It was the last gift he ever donated to the Englishman who rarely failed, during their many later encounters, to get up Miller's nose and rejoiced in doing so.

Bailey still had a lot to learn, and he knew it. During the 1947 season, he had been unwise enough to mention, during the tea interval, to Tom Pearce, his bluff, burly captain, that he had never conceded 100 runs off his bowling in one innings. 'Then you aren't a bowler yet,' said Tom. (Trevor's bowling analysis at the time stood at one wicket for 94 runs). 'Take the first over after tea.' Trevor duly did so. Pearce standing at first slip, counted off the runs, rather too loudly for comfort until Trevor reached his 'ton'. One part of his education was complete.

It was a learning process which, according to Ray Smith, the seasoned Essex all-rounder, was given impetus during that 1948 Australian match. Talking to me over a pint of bitter in the Grand Hotel at Leicester during my own first away match for the county, some six years after the Southend massacre, Ray was in expansive mood.

'All the bowling came alike to the Aussies that day,' said Ray, 'and to no one more obviously than Bradman. Tom Pearce, our skipper, had rung the changes before lunch, but our only success while they put on nearly 250 runs in that time, came when I managed, with devilish cunning, to get Sid Barnes to tread on his wicket when he had made 79. Bradman was only in for a few minutes before lunch, and Tom decided, reasonably enough, to give Frank Vigar, our looping leg-spinner, a psychological last over at the Don. Frank was never one to push the ball through but he did spin it. He had a good leg-break, two types of googly and a top-spinner, and he ran through his repertoire during his first five balls at the great man. They all pitched on a reasonable length.

'The only problem was that Don hit all five balls for four. Worse, he hit them all off the back foot, in exactly the same place, past mid-on with that pull shot of his which never lifted the ball more than an inch off the ground. Then he played the last ball back to the bowler, tucked his gloves and his bat under his arm and ambled off for lunch. I could see Trevor massaging his chin and raising his eyebrows while all this was going on. He had already taken nought for plenty and must have been wondering what was in store in the afternoon. He had bowled pretty fast that morning, and it seemed that the faster he bowled, the faster the ball went to the boundary, and our catching, especially in the slips, had not exactly assisted him.

'Anyhow, it was mid-afternoon, Brown and Bradman had both made hundreds, and Trevor was plainly becoming more and more fed up, when Brown top-edged a ball off his bowling. The ball went straight up in the air, and Frank Rist, our wicket-keeper, standing some ten yards back, advanced to get under it. Others made movements in a similar direction. But as the ball hovered, so Trevor decided that this was one that would not get away. "Mine," he shouted, waving aside everyone in his vision, and he set off down the wicket. What he hadn't realised was that the wind was taking the ball away from him with

24

every stride he took and he finished flat out past the batsman's wicket, having dived full-length, with still a yard to go before reaching the place where the ball eventually landed.' (In fact, this incident occurred later and in another place. It was just that Ray liked to tell the story that way after a beer or two.)

Even less palatable for Trevor was the fact that a broken finger caused him to miss the chance of batting against the Australians. However, it was as a result of this match that Trevor Bailey became the bowler of searching line and length at a fast-medium pace, with a natural out-swinger, occasional break-back and a full command over where the ball was going, who was to make one of the most successful all-rounders England has ever had.

He came back to Cambridge, as Insole says, 'mumbling something to the effect that if he had placed his field properly and bowled intelligently he could have cut down the runs by half.' It was then that he decided to cut down one of the 'whirls' in his action. Later, he was to run up at an angle to the stumps so as to get closeer to them, his left foot landing in front of the non-striking batsman's leg stump for the out-swinger – but always varying the angle of delivery, experimenting with the grip. It was then that sheer application made him, with Alec Bedser, one of the most accurate bowlers in England. It also enabled a slender frame to cope with the demands of batting, bowling and fielding for long spells. It made him a better, more durable cricketer.

But that was to come. What had already happened was to ensure that he could continue to play cricket for Essex, and possibly for England, for the foreseeable future. It also meant that he could remain an amateur, although there were many who thought it hardly meant that, and that he was being paid to play cricket while hanging on to the tatters of an amateur status.

Before the end of an unsettled and unsettling year for him, he had come to an arrangement with Essex. The following is distilled from the Essex CCC minutes of the time and contemporaneous accounts and reported in *Essex County Cricket Club: the Complete History* by David Lemmon and Mike Marshall. It is as an objective and factual account as one is likely to find.

'At the beginning of the 1948 season an approach was made to the chairman [Lt-Col. Hubert Ashton] with a view to [Bailey] joining the club in some capacity which would enable him to devote his full time to playing first-class cricket after coming down from Cambridge. An ad-hoc committee, consisting of the chairman and other committee members, had a meeting with Trevor Bailey, when the whole matter was discussed in detail. As a result, a proposal was made to Bailey, subject to approval by the council. This entailed Bailey assuming the position of assistant secretary and provided for mutual co-operation between the secretary, R. F. T. Paterson, and Bailey. A special council meeting was held at which the ad-hoc committee's report and proposals were fully considered. It was pointed out by the ad-hoc committee that it must be realised that in present circumstances fewer and fewer amateurs could afford to play throughout a season without some assistance directly or indirectly . . . The ad-hoc committee also felt that the council should consider carefully before losing the services of a man with Bailey's potential abilities on the cricket field and, in time, with guidance, off the field also. After further lengthy discussion it was decided to offer T. E. Bailey a three-year agreement as from 1st October 1948. These were submitted to, and accepted by, T. E. Bailey.'

Trevor puts it this way: 'Essex offered me a post as assistant secretary, which allowed me to play first-class cricket for the whole of the summer and increased my chances of making an overseas tour with MCC. It also allowed me to go on teaching during the two winter terms, as my duties with Essex at the time were not too demanding. The outcome was, I returned to Alleyn Court for two wonderful winters.'

Trevor was finding out what it was like to have his cake and eat it, and if there were a number of professional cricketers who thoroughly resented this type of 'shamateurism' they kept it mainly in-house. That some did resent it and later showed it cannot be in doubt.

2

On his Way to the Top

1948–52

The 1949 season was a celebratory one. It was a celebration of Bailey's talent, a celebration that he was at last settled domestically, a celebration of the fact that, in so far as cricket provided security, he had it. With a three-year contract in the safe at county headquarters, albeit for an assistant secretary's job, his career as a cricketer was assured. Futhermore, he would travel first-class all the way.

In addition, his appearances for the amateur football club, Leytonstone, during the winter had sharpened his reflexes, increased his stamina and swelled his bank account by more than just reasonable expenses. He had been well advised, in every way – not least financially – to turn down the offer to go to West Indies with the forty-five-year-old Gubby Allen's ill-fated venture in 1947–48; he had instead increased his standing in a football world where amateurs often received more financial reward than professionals. A successful winter in 1948–49 had left him as fit as a fiddle and at ease with himself in every facet of his life.

It showed on the cricket field; my word, it did. As a bowler, he made the best of all possible beginnings. Essex played MCC in the first match of the season at Lord's. Running in for his first ball of the first-class season, his action better controlled because of the elimination of one of his 'whirls', seventeen paces leading to a high, arching leap before delivery, Bailey bowled the first ball of the match to Nigel Howard. An outswinger, it found the unfortunate Howard groping hesitantly, found the edge of the bat, found the sanctuary of Wade's big, gloved hands behind the wicket, and set Bailey off on a memorable year.

Five wickets in the match, 103 runs in his two innings, including 82 in the first, and his first full season with Essex was up and running.

Later, describing himself as a cricketer in that golden summer, Bailey says:

'I was a fast-medium bowler – not fast in the Lindwall-Miller sense, but sharp enough to be able to send down a reasonable bouncer, to obtain the odd wicket through pace alone and to make the tail-ender slightly apprehensive. I relied largely on the out-swinger and the 'nip-backer' but, although I had gained greater smoothness through cutting out a whirl in my action, it was still not completely grooved and I had not yet attained the control required, nor had I sufficiently studied opposing batsmen. I was not yet a *thinking bowler*. As a result, there were occasions in both the Tests and county matches when I was too expensive. However, my striking rate was high, which was the main reason, apart from a lack of competition, why I opened the bowling for England.

'As for my batting, I had become a dependable middle-order batsman with Essex, who expected to score more than 1,000 runs in a full summer with an average of over 30. If, at this time, I had concentrated entirely on batting and claimed a permanent place higher in the Essex order I could have made more runs, but I would not have been picked to play against New Zealand. Anyway, I would never have found the game so satisfying if I had become only an occasional bowler.

'In addition to being an all-rounder, I was also an all round fieldsman. I have always enjoyed fielding, until one day at Leyton towards the end of my career when I stood at slip and dropped catch after catch off my two unfortunate spinners. However, in 1949, I was equally at home in the deep, the covers, the slips, or backward short-leg, which was a useful asset, especially in international cricket.'

However that may have been, the figures that season spoke for themselves. Bailey played in all four Test matches against the New Zealanders; but, before that, he had encountered them at Lord's when playing for MCC in late May. On the first day, in front of 25,000 people, MCC had made 311 for 4 wickets. On the Monday, after his team had added 60-odd to that total, Bailey took 4 of the first six New Zealand wickets to fall while they scored only 96, uprooting the off stump of Bert Sutcliffe, the prolific left-hander, and removing his old adversary, Martin Donnelly, to a fine slip catch by Bill Edrich when he had made only 9. New Zealand recovered some measure of pride, but not before Bailey had etched himself on the memory with a most brilliant diving catch at short-leg to get rid of Mervyn Wallace – a catch singled out by *Wisden* as the highlight of the match.

The taking of 12 wickets for 141 while playing for MCC against Surrey at Lord's shortly after his *tour de force* against MCC for Essex, had already been a stepping-stone to Test-match cricket before his performance against the New Zealanders sealed the issue. In those days, more than now, when scouts travel the length and breadth of the country, a performance at Lord's was always reckoned to be worth two or three anywhere else. Well, three such performances at headquarters before the end of May simply could not be ignored, and Bailey's selection for the first Test at Leeds, starting on 11th June, was a formality. No nervous young *ingénu*, Trevor rose to the occasion. He was easily England's most successful bowler with 6 wickets for 118 from thirty-two overs, a fine analysis on a perfect pitch. New Zealand had been allocated only three days for each of the four Test matches, and they were keen to show that they were worth more than that. They were giving nothing away, packing their Test teams with batting, determined not to lose. They had high-class players and, as an emerging country, they wanted the world to know it. The pitches throughout the series remained good for batting. And, in fact, each match in the series was drawn. England bowled a lot of overs, and Bailey bowled more than his fair share of them: 158 in the four matches (only Eric Hollies, the Warwickshire leg-spinner, bowled marginally more), and his 16 wickets were six more than any other bowler.

If his bowling at this stage of his career was the most prized aspect of his game – and he was faster than anyone playing regularly in the first-class game that season – his batting was almost as successful, and frequently eye-catching. Those were the days before his main claim to fame was as a limpet at the crease. *Wisden*, when assessing him as one of their five cricketers-of-the-year for 1949, had this to say about his batting: 'Bailey is a capable No. 5 or 6 batsman. He would be quite content to play sound, steady cricket, but circumstances have tended to make him an aggressive player. He is an attractive stroke-player with a fondness for the cut, but can score quite freely with the drive and leg-side strokes.'

Harry Gee, whose initials appear at the end of the piece on Trevor, could be said to have described the position accurately enough in 1949. If at the end of the series you had asked Walter Hadlee, the New Zealand captain, he would have agreed with the assessment. Bailey had scored but 12 in his one Test innings before the second Test at Lord's. But now . . .

England had lost their first 5 wickets for 112 runs on the first day when Trevor joined Denis Compton. He was quickly off the mark, turning two stray balls from the tiring Jack Cowie for four. It was a hot day, and Compton had been in for some time. Now he was completely outdone. Oozing confidence, in front a full house at headquarters where he had flourished without exception that season, Bailey unfurled a range of strokes which brought him ten fours in his first 50, hoisted after he had been at the crease for little more than an hour. As Compton followed suit, producing some incomparable shots of his own once England were out of trouble, Bailey adopted a supporting role. Even so, he had been in for only two and a half hours when, on 93, he cut Geoff Rabone hard to the wicket-keeper's foot and second slip caught the rebound.

In a long career in which he was to play eighty-nine more Test-match innings, Bailey made only one century. All contemporary accounts agree that this time not only did he richly deserve to make one, but that it would have been as good a hundred as was made all season. Not that his contribution with the ball caused him to do much singing in the bath. The dreaded Martin Donnelly cut loose during the second hundred of his 206 runs and Trevor, who bowled thirty-three overs (again, second only to Hollies), took none for 136 and suffered more than anybody (*see* Appendix 2).

It was a different story at Old Trafford where, for two of the three days, England had the best of it, although the difference did not extend to much variation in the way Donnelly treated Bailey. But this time Bailey suffered only for a brief period – it included one over which cost 16 runs – by which time he was flagging towards the end of a fine spell of bowling. Freddie Brown had put in New Zealand, and Bailey had taken 3 wickets for 11 runs in eleven overs while the opposition lurched to 82 for 4 at lunch. Six wickets for 84 was Trevor's haul in the first innings. He also made an undefeated 72 in England's only innings, indulging in a long partnership with Nottinghamshire's Reg Simpson. It was the beginning of what was to become a lifelong friendship between the two.

By the time the final Test match arrived in mid-August, Bailey's immense stamina had been well and truly put to the test. He acquitted himself well enough in that final match with runs and wickets but, by then, even his Test-match performances had been to some extent overshadowed. For in between Test matches he had been knocking off the runs and mowing down the wickets for Essex to such effect that, on 1st August, he completed the double of 1,000 runs and 100 wickets. He was easily the first to achieve that feat in a season which saw only Brian Close, Roly Jenkins and Freddie Brown join him past that particular post.

All told, Trevor scored nearly 1,400 runs and took 130 wickets that year. Ten of those wickets had come his way during a single innings against Lancashire. The taking of all 10 happens to few cricketers in the course of a career, and there is inevitably a bit of luck about it. Or, more precisely, bad luck in the case of the other bowlers on the side who do not muster a single wicket between them. One thinks particularly of Jim Laker's 19 wickets in a match against the 1956 Australians as the supreme example of this. On that occasion, Tony Lock, a great spinner in his own right, was bowling his heart out, striving might and main, right to the end, to get wickets.

Bailey's achievement was not quite like that. Essex were playing Lancashire at Clacton on a good wicket. Runs were plentiful during Clacton week that year and Lancashire, having won the toss, made 331. Bailey took 10 wickets for 90 runs in 39.4 overs. The bowling of nearly forty overs in a day was unusual even then. So too, it seems, were the methods employed towards the end of Lancashire's innings. Bailey's away-swinger had been going late and often that day. Six of his wickets were caught by the wicket-keeper or in the slip region. The others were bowled.

Bailey says that he never really considered the prospect of taking all 10 wickets until very late in the innings. By then he had taken 6 wickets, and only the tail remained. 'It was not until two more had come my way after tea that I, or anyone else, recognised the possibility. But I could never have captured the final two without the active co-operation of Tom Pearce who, in the closing stages, used two non-bowlers, including himself, whose purpose was not to get a wicket. The objective was to do everything possible to help me. The fact that the Lancashire tail scored rather more runs than they should have done he regarded as immaterial.'

Bailey feels that, if his great friend, Doug Insole, had been captain on that day as he often was later, he would never have taken all 10 because there would have been no help at the other end. Certainly, he would have had to earn them the hard way – Insole would never have allowed personal success for anyone to get in the way of bowling out Lancashire as cheaply as possible. As captain of Cambridge he once declared on John Dewes and Hubert Doggart when they were 27 runs short of a world second-wicket record. But that is another story.

In 1949 Bailey played fifty first-class innings, twelve fewer than Bill Edrich, who played more than anybody, but within a few of most regular county openers. He also bowled 1,200 overs – more than Alec Bedser, more than many a regular opening bowler on the county circuit. Only five bowlers took more wickets; he was the supreme bowler/batsman all-rounder of that year, and in the context of the times he was in his pomp. Yet he knew that modifications to his bowling action were necessary. He recognised that, while his speed was a potent weapon in an era where genuine, English fast bowlers were non-existent, more craft and less speed would probably be needed if he were to hold his own in the England team for years to come when one or two genuine fast bowlers came along. He had seen Lindwall and Miller,

Essex v Lancashire at Clacton. August 24, 25 1949

Lancashire

C. Washbrook c Wade b Bailey	18		
J. T. Ikin b Bailey	42		
W. Place c Wade b Bailey	28		
G. A. Edrich c Vigar b Bailey	82		
K. Grieves c Wade b Bailey	11		
N. D. Howard c Vigar b Bailey	66		
P. Greenwood c Vigar b Bailey	2		
J. H. G. Deighton c Pearce b Bailey	1		
R. Tattersall not out	34	— not out	3
W. B. Roberts b Bailey	15		
A. Barlow b Bailey	12	— not out	0
B 10, l-b 9, w 1	20		
	311	(No wkt.)	3

Essex

T. C. Dodds c Grieves b Deighton	11	— b Greenwood	37
S. J. Cray c Ikin b Deighton	10	— b Deighton	6
F. H. Vigar c Barlow b Grieves	53	— c Deighton b Roberts	10
R. Horsfall c Edrich b Greenwood	11	— b Greenwood	19
T. E. Bailey c Ikin b Greenwood	10	— c Barlow b Tattersall	28
T. N. Pearce run out	28	— b Roberts	12
W. B. Morris c Edrich b Deighton	13	— c Ikin b Roberts	15
R. Smith c Ikin b Greenwood	6	— st Barlow b Roberts	20
T. P. B. Smith c Barlow b Deighton	0	— b Roberts	7
T. H. Wade c Barlow b Deighton	1	— b Roberts	0
E. J. Price not out	3	— not out	1
B 7, l-b 7, n-b 4	18	B 12, l-b 2	14
	164		169

Essex Bowling

	O.	M.	R.	W.	O.	M.	R.	W.
Bailey	39.4	9	90	10				
R. Smith	33	8	107	0				
P. Smith	12	3	26	0				
Vigar	7	1	27	0				
Price	8	1	29	0				
Morris	3	1	12	0				
Pearce	4	0	20	0				
Wade					0.3	0	3	0

Lancashire Bowling

	O.	M.	R.	W.		O.	M.	R.	W.
Greenwood	24	4	38	3	....	19	5	47	2
Deighton	24	3	53	5	....	11	2	30	1
Tattersall	7	1	15	0	....	9	2	27	1
Roberts	16	7	18	0	....	22.4	8	29	6
Grieves	8	2	22	1	....	8	3	22	0

Umpires: C. N. Woolley and K. McCanlis.

33

knew what fast bowling was, and knew he did not fit that category. Still, as we have seen, he had not yet by any means come to the stage where his batting had become an exercise in self-denial; he had not even considered the possibility. He had played some stubborn innings that year. But he was essentially a free spirit with a wide range of strokes, often used to advantage.

Essex were proud of him. The taking of all 10 wickets against Lancashire was marked by a formal presentation of the ball, mounted and suitably inscribed. The ceremony was performed by Lt-Col. Hubert Ashton, a former amateur with Essex, and at that time the club's president and Member of Parliament for Chelmsford. In those days before MPs were quite the figures of fun they are today, he was greatly respected in Essex and elsewhere. He was also a tireless worker on behalf of the club and he was pleased with his efforts to ensure that Bailey and Essex were now insolubly linked.

Linked, that is, during the summer months. For that winter, with no MCC tour scheduled (there was not a tour every winter at that time – and it was a matter of deliberate policy) Trevor turned again to Alleyn Court and his other great love: association football. He had good connections within the game. His father-in-law was a director of Southend United, he himself had played with Southend reserves, had enjoyed a successful season with Leytonstone. He was a scorer of goals and a drifter away from defences, well able to hold his own in the highest reaches of the amateur game. But, typically, he had no illusions about his limitations. He played for Leytonstone at centre-forward and, with his remarkable capacity for honest self-analysis when he assesses his ability at any game, he will tell you that he was never a genuine centre-forward. He will point to his being neither strong enough nor proficient enough in the air. He rates his best asset, when with Leytonstone, as being a useful decoy for their chief goal-scorer, Alf Noble. His left foot, he will tell you, was a swinger and not much more. His tackling was not a strong suit. Against that, he will admit to being quick off the mark, and fast over twenty yards; a good reader of the game with a knack for being in the right place at the right time; an accurate corner-kicker.

This is all a bit self-deprecating, though. He had mixed it with the professionals when in the Marines and had continued to improve his game, although the spasmodic nature of the fixtures and exigencies of the service in war-time had limited his opportunities and his progress. It was his time at Cambridge that had whetted his appetite and polished his skills, and gave him an unquenchable thirst for success. When Cambridge beat Oxford in 1946, the *Sunday Times* headlined their report the 'Best University Match for Years':

'Not since the days of Norman Creek, the Ashtons and A. G. Doggart – nearby a quarter of a century ago – has there been a better inter-varsity soccer match, from the point of view of sheer football skill, than that played on Dulwich Hamlet's ground yesterday. Cambridge won, and deservedly, by virtue of their speedier and better combined forward play . . .

'The important fact emerges that soccer in the universities is very much on the up-grade. For long periods hardly a pass was wasted, and even in the most exciting moments the players never succumbed to the temptation to sacrifice skill for the purpose of engaging in hard kicking and ruthless spoiling tactics . . .

'All the Cambridge forwards excelled, and Trevor Bailey played the game of his life . . . Both sides attacked in turn for long periods, and play became very exciting as the game developed. Cambridge were on top in the early stages, and it was against the run of play when Tanner put Oxford ahead after twenty-two minutes with a magnificent goal. Then Crawford equalised following great work by Trevor Bailey on the other wing.

'Play had barely resumed when Tanner put Oxford ahead again, and they then held the initiative. However, Cambridge suddenly rallied, and their fowards made a desperate and successful bid to win the match. Foxall gave Weir no chance for their second, and Trevor Bailey scored their winning goal with eight minutes to go.'

Those were the great days of university sport. At association football, cricket and rugby, the university players were capable of playing at the highest level, and many of them went on to do so. In Trevor's time at Cambridge, there were several double cricket and soccer Blues, and still greater honours afterwards for the likes of Tony Pawson and Donald Carr of Oxford, while Cambridge had in Hubert Doggart, Doug Insole and Trevor Bailey three similar tyros of both games. It was in his first soccer trial at Cambridge that Trevor began his friendship – and partnership – with Doug Insole; Insole was at inside-right, Bailey on the right wing in that trial, and later in the match against Oxford. Insole remembers being impressed by the perceptive skills on the football field of his partner in the forward line who had been to a rugby school and was known to him only by his reputation as a formidable cricketer.

Times change. In those days, the Amateur Cup final would draw a capacity crowd. Playing for Leytonstone meant playing in front of at least 5,000 people in an Isthmian League match, and nearly double that number in an early round of the Amateur Cup. A replayed Cup semi-final defeat was the nearest Bailey came to a Wembley Cup final in his Leytonstone days, but he loved it – the whole scene – and he gloried in his fitness without making a fetish of it. He has always been one for a good party.

But even Bailey's young muscles were liable to strain. The 1950 cricket season was a painful reminder of that. It turned out to be a good year by anyone's standards but it did have its drawbacks – 'snags', as Bailey would invariably call them, after the most careful consideration and a wrinkling of the nose. Injuries to the groin and back plagued him after a wonderful start to the season. Two a penny in the modern game, such strains were comparatively rare in the early 1950s, perhaps because the pros in those days often bowled through injuries in order to keep a place in the side and thus not lose all-important match-money. Amateurs could be more choosy – which is not to cast aspersions on the nature of Bailey's injuries, which prevented him bowling for spells during that 1950 season and restricted his appearances in Test matches against West Indies to two. He had played at Cambridge against the

36

1948 Australians, knowing that he was not fully fit; had broken a finger in the early stages of the match against the same tourists at Southend and had continued to bowl and field throughout the day. He had learned that sub-standard performances through carrying an injury were seldom in the best interests of his team, or himself.

So, whereas 1949 had seen him plot a trouble-free course through all those innings and all those overs, 1950 restricted his appearances. When playing for Essex he could play as a batsman. For England it was as an all-rounder that he earned his place and had built his reputation.

The season began promisingly. Four wickets in thirty overs against Northamptonshire, following a successful bowl against his old university, found everything in good working order. He was stumped by Ken Fiddling in the Northants match, and that did not happen often; but he avoided the most dreaded dismissal of all which, in those days, was caught Fiddling bowled Nutter. Then, in the second match of the Brentwood week, in mid-May against Glamorgan, he had, even for him, a most remarkable bowling performance. Bailey, 1bw b E. Davies 0, was a line in the scorecard which did not best please him. This was especially the case since his team-mates had batted with some abandon to run up a total of 384 in reply to Glamorgan's first-innings 167. Glamorgan had reached 81 for 2 in their second innings by tea on the second day when the hitherto wicketless Bailey decided the time had come to slip himself. The pitch was slightly worn, and Bailey, bowling fast, caused apprehension in the ranks of the Welshmen. In one ball more than five overs, Trevor took 7 wickets for 3 runs. In fact, from the time he took his first wicket, by removing Stan Montgomery's middle stump, he took all these wickets without a run being scored off his bowling. It will rank forever as one of the great wicket-to-wicket spells. Well, you can hardly do better than take 7 for 0.

The visitors that year were the West Indians. It was to be the year of Weekes, Worrell and Walcott; the year of 'those two little pals of mine, Ramadin and Valentine'. But nobody was to know that. West Indies had never won a Test match, let alone a series, in England, but the mauling dealt to G. O. Allen's team in 1947–48 had shown that they had some world-class individual players. The three W's had been in the runs, and the side was a cohesive force, for once, under John Goddard's influence. Unlike other West Indies teams, they carried players able to perform in all kinds of conditions.

The Old Trafford Test was the first in the series. The matches this year were each of five days' duration, but for some time it scarcely looked as though three would be needed to bring this match to a conclusion. To begin with, the ball turned from the word 'go', the bounce was unpredictable, and Norman Yardley, having left out Alec Bedser for a spinner, was relieved to win the toss and bat. His feelings took a nose-dive when Alf Valentine, the West Indies slow left-arm bowler, took the ball and began turning it just enough to find the edge. From 51 for no wicket, England subsided to 88 for 5, with Hutton in the pavilion nursing a badly bruised hand, having retired hurt. Valentine sat down to lunch having bowled seventeen overs and taken all 5 wickets for 34 runs.

Bailey had been joined by Godfrey Evans, and the two of them not only set a new sixth-wicket record partnership of 161 in matches between the two sides, but completely turned the course of the match. Because Evans was naturally a perky if somewhat vulnerable stroke-player and showed no intention of departing from his normal plan of attack, Bailey decided to play a defensive role, to drop anchor and to employ the forward defensive which was later to become his trademark. It was, in fact, here that the 'Barnacle' was probably born, although the birth was not yet seen for what it was. What was recognised was a defensive innings of the highest quality, as he scored an undefeated 82 in over three and a half hours. While he and Evans were at the wicket together, Evans scored 2 runs to every 1 by Trevor but, once in the groove, Bailey simply plodded on, stern defence occasionally relieved by the punishment of anything too short to worry him.

Bailey also played a large part in England's second innings. He made 33 in over two hours at the crease after England had again wilted early in the face of Ramadhin and Valentine. England won the match with plenty to spare, and to Bailey went much of the credit, although muscular problems were to cause him to miss the second Test at Lord's, the ground where he invariably did well.

By then, the likeable Tom Pearce had resigned in mid-term from the Essex captaincy, an event which created some turmoil in Trevor's well-ordered mind. He had grown used to Tom and his mildly eccentric ways. This year, though, Essex were in the doldrums; results had found them grounded near the bottom of the table, with few signs of any dynamic to pull themselves up. Tom Pearce himself was also far from his best. Captain, either solely or jointly, since 1933, he was now a Test selector. It had been agreed that the 1950 season should see a joint arrangement between himself and Doug Insole, fresh from Cambridge, a batsman almost, but never quite, in the highest class as a Test player. But this was an arrangement which caused some heart-searching. When Pearce elected to give up his joint captaincy in mid-season, it came as something of a shock. Bailey maintains to this day that he never seriously entertained the notion that the mantle of captaincy would fall upon him, claiming that he remained largely oblivious of the nuances around him. Certainly, in retrospect, he realises that he was not the man for the job at that stage of his career: too concerned with his own performance; intolerant of anyone whom he judged to be unwilling or unable to give to the game the same degree of devotion as he was. 'Unlike Doug,' he says, 'I have never been a political animal, have always lacked discretion. It has never worried me that what I said or did upset somebody who was likely to be useful in the future.'

Bailey claims also to have recognised that Insole as a batsman, not a bowler like himself, nor paid as he was by Essex, would be in a better position to make a success of the captaincy. Then, again, the amateur system prevalent at the time made Insole's transition from without relatively painless – which is not to say that there was no chuntering from the senior pros such as the Smiths, Peter and Ray, and Tom Wade, the long-serving wicket-keeper.

These were unhappy times at Essex. Trevor, for all his apparent aloofness from what was happening, admits to being at odds with the manner of Pearce's departure. 'It simply confirmed my view that it was stupid to trust any committee or political body.' But he was to become a great admirer of Insole's ability both as a batsman and as captain. Certain it is that Insole never failed to consult Bailey on any tactical aspects of the game when the two were in the same team, just as it cannot be denied that Bailey's input into the decision-making process was never than less than 51 per cent. Great friends on and off the field in years to come, the Insole/Bailey axis became inviolate and served Essex well.

But as Essex, despite all the shenanigans, were unable to move themselves from the bottom of the table, Bailey was having his own problems, largely of a physical nature, as recurrent back problems continued to plague him. He was to learn, quite by chance, a remedy for the back strains brought about by long spells of fast bowling. A casual conversation with Reg Perks, the Worcestershire fast bowler, renowned both for his ability to move the ball off the seam from leg to off and for a penchant for wheeling through long spells without apparent strain, set Bailey on the right track. Perks suggested that Bailey follow his example. 'Wear a vest,' he said, 'and borrow one of your wife's roll-ons. It will give your back just the support it needs.' Following this advice had its drawbacks. Trevor cut off the suspenders, but it was difficult to avoid a certain amount of ribaldry in the dressing-room when he first produced this new article of essential equipment, although nobody quite dared suggest that the T in T. E. Bailey stood for Transvestite.

Meanwhile, one of the world's great calypsos had been born. *Housewife's Choice*, one of the popular programmes of the time, was inundated with requests for Lord Kitchener's *Lord's Calypso*. 'Rae knew the Queen had come to see/So he started off with a century.' Or, 'Our bowling really was superfine/With Ramadhin and Valentine.' Ramadhin took 11 wickets in the second Test; Valentine took 7. Victory at Lord's, and the manner of it, added up to a momentous boost for West Indies in the four-match series, putting them all-square with two matches to play; and folk were beginning to take them seriously.

Bailey had dropped out of the Lord's Test at virtually the last moment. He showed little real form between then and the third match at Nottingham, either through absence because of injury, or inability to bowl through injury, and was not selected for a match which left West Indies winners by 10 wickets. It did Bailey no harm to sit this one out:

Worrell made 261 runs; Weekes 129; the West Indies' first innings total of 558 was the highest by either side in England; Worrell's was the highest Test score by a batsman of either side in an England v West Indies match in England. And so it went on.

So did Bailey, but mostly he was on the massage table. His propensity for a quick rub-down was behind a minor *cause célèbre* when Essex were playing Sussex at Clacton. *Wisden* reported as follows:

'Bailey, when bowling, was the central figure in a remarkable happening on the first day. Having sent down six overs for 8 runs he went off for attention for pain in the shoulder and neck. On his return he prepared to bowl, but James Langridge, the Sussex captain, went to the middle and consulted with the Essex captain and the umpires as to whether Bailey, who had received massage during half an hour off the field, should be allowed to bowl at once. It was decided that he should not be used again for an hour. Langridge stated that he raised the point as one of principle and that he himself would not re-employ for at least an hour any of his bowlers if they were involved in a similar occurrence.'

Throughout his career Bailey was to be a central figure in happenings which later caused change in the game's legislation. Not because of this incident, but because of many other incidents which followed, the law was introduced which prevented anyone bowling after treatment until he had fulfilled at least a similar time on the field as he had spent off it. The interesting and original use of substitutes (among other things) by the Pakistanis on their 1992 tour may well have the law-makers scratching their heads again. My own report on their match against Northamptonshire in *The Times* of 15th June 1992 illustrates the point:

'Wasim Akram was in devastating form, in spite of having been denied an early rub-down on Saturday evening by a gesticulating Northamptonshire last man, Nick Cook, who apparently wanted to know why he was leaving the field at the end of a spell which brought him 3 for 24 off nine overs with no apparent pain. Cook's objections were supported by umpire Wight, and Akram stayed on, shrugging the while. The incident would appear to have had no lasting effect on the general Pakistan view of these things. Both [Salim] Malik and Inzamam, having stroked the ball around with no apparent trouble, failed to appear when Pakistan took the field, various substitutes fielding in place of them. Doubtless both will be in rare fettle at Lord's.'

Although doubts about Bailey's resilience and stamina were given wide circulation during that summer of 1950, he played in the fourth and final Test at the Oval, bowled well enough, and scored a few, but not many, runs. But neither he nor anyone else – not even Len Hutton with 202 not out – could do much to prevent West Indies winning by an innings. West Indies had found themselves. Gone were the days when anything but England's best would survive against them, let alone prevail.

In spite of the question-marks now against his name, Trevor finished the season with just over 1,000 runs and 88 wickets, and was selected to go to Australia and New Zealand with Freddie Brown's MCC team of 1950–51. It was touch and go as to whether he would be chosen. As *Wisden* noted, before the tour Bailey was far from being everybody's nominee. But then nor were several others who took part in that tour, and Bailey's Test-match record thus far in his career was superior to that of many who were selected. In the event, his performances were to mark a recovery stage in a career that had stumbled. They confirmed his promise as a world-class all-round cricketer, as an opening bowler who batted, and as a cricketer who could lift his game when the stakes were at their highest. He also broke a thumb. This unfortunately confirmed his susceptibility to injury.

The emphasis laid by the selectors on youth and relative in-experience was the subject of much adverse comment both before and after the series. Cambridge was well to the fore in the shape of John Dewes, David Sheppard and John Warr; the sole orthodox spinner was the left-armer, Bob Berry of Lancashire (twenty-four and a fledgling in the craft), unless you count Brian Close, a batsman-bowler at the age of nineteen who bowled off-spin but was hardly in Jim Laker's class. Laker was left behind, along with Bill Edrich and Jack Robertson of Middlesex and a number of other prolific and experienced batsmen. With Denis Compton barely recovered from a series of knee operations, there was an unwarranted softness about the middle order. The team contained three leg-spinners: Doug Wright, Eric Hollies and Brown himself. The new-ball attack was in the hands of Alec Bedser, a giant in every way, Bailey and Warr, who was promising with 87 wickets to his name in 1950, but scarcely proven.

Bailey's proneness to injury did not improve the outlook, especially when muscular ailments in his shoulder prevented him from bowling properly either in Colombo on the way out to Australia, or in the nets when the party arrived in Perth. Almost before the tour had started, the British press were seriously suggesting that Bailey, Berry and Warr should be sent home. Work done by an Australian physiotherapist enabled Bailey to resume full fitness, after which there was never a suggestion that he be sent home. The luckless Berry and Warr never really justified their selection, however, any more than Gilbert Parkhouse, Dewes or Sheppard; while poor Brian Close, having fallen foul of Freddie Brown, had a tour he wanted quickly to forget.

In all the circumstances, Brown's team did remarkably well to win one of the five Test matches. It owed much to the indomitable Freddie, who overcame a shortage in the seam department by bowling medium-pace himself. England had belied all previous expectations by bowling out Australia in the first Test at Brisbane for 228 on a good wicket thanks to Bailey and Bedser. But they experienced far the worst of the pitch after rain had caused the development of a typical Wagga sticky wicket, and they were defeated. Seven wickets in the match for Bailey worked wonders for his confidence, and at Melbourne in the second Test he again bowled with great life and precision for a match analysis of 6 for 87, in a low-scoring game which England lost by only 28 runs. Freddie Brown's little medium-pace seamers had also been both economical and destructive on a wicket in which large cracks appeared, and it seemed the England side had discovered a new weapon.

Little did anyone realise how badly England would need Brown's bowling in the third Test at Sydney. This time it was a perfect batting pitch; Brown won the toss (the only time in seven Test matches, including those in New Zealand, that he was to do so) and batted. He scored 79 himself, but England had not made the most of their opportunity, thanks to some fine bowling by Miller, when Bailey came to the wicket at 187 for 5 wickets. Bailey helped Brown to put on 71 runs, but a lifting ball from Lindwall fractured his right thumb. Having retired hurt, Bailey came back twice to resume his innings, the second time with his thumb in plaster. He actually batted in the second innings, too, but there was no way he could bowl. He was condemned to watch as Doug Wright, the Kent leg-spinner, tore a muscle running between the wickets: and later, while England, reduced to virtually three bowlers (Bedser, Brown and Warr), had over 400 taken off them by the Australians, finally losing the match by an innings. The three remaining bowlers had bowled 123 overs between them; Brown and Bedser took 4 wickets each; Warr finished with none for 142 after a valiant effort, bowling turn and turn about with Bedser and Brown from mid-afternoon on Saturday, all through Monday, until lunchtime on Tuesday.

It was on that Tuesday lunchtime that Warr says he was approached unsteadily by an Australian who had spent the morning sampling Foster's finest product and was feeling the effects of the hot sun as well. 'Tell me, Mr Warr,' he said, 'do you think you'll ever take a wicket in a Test match in Australia?' Not to be drawn, Warr replied that he thought he would. Provided he was picked for the next Test, he fancied his chances. 'Mr Warr,' said the man, swaying ever so slightly, 'you've got as much chance of taking a wicket in a Test match in Australia as I've got of stuffing a pound of butter up a parrot's bum with a red-hot needle.' He was wrong. Warr got a wicket in the fourth Test.

Bailey was off the injured list in time to play in the fifth Test match and to savour the first victory over the Australians by an England team since the war. By then he had been out of action for more than a month, but had made a century on his return against Victoria, his thumb still bandaged. He contributed comparatively little to England's victory in the final Test, but made another, undefeated, century – his only one in international cricket – in the first of the Tests in New Zealand, and he also captured his fair share of wickets. He returned from the tour disappointed to a degree, but with his reputation justly enhanced. He had also enjoyed himself, sensibly, but perhaps slightly too much. The combination of two boat trips – to and from Australia – and the none-too-abstemious way of life in the Antipodes found him tipping the scales more than a stone heavier than when the odyssey began.

He also returned a more complete player than when he had left for Australia. If he had not been sufficient of a 'thinking' bowler when he set out at the end of the 1950 season, he was by the time he finished that tour. Although able to bowl only seventy-five overs in the Australian Test matches, he had taken 14 wickets at just over 14 runs apiece and had impressed by his ability to direct his attack according to the individual strengths and weaknesses of his opponents. In a quest for the Ashes that was the most notable for the 21-wicket success of Jack Iverson, the 'freak' Australian spinner who, with uncanny accuracy, spun the ball off the top of the middle finger of his right hand – a trick he had learned in a Japanese prisoner-of-war camp – the quite brilliant and consistent batsmanship of Len Hutton, and the abject failure of poor Denis Compton, Bailey's determination, in the words of *Wisden*, 'won him many new friends'.

Yet, in spite of this, the next two years were to see him play in only two Test matches, both against South Africa in 1951. He missed three Tests that year; was not picked for any of the four home Tests against India in 1952; was, like so many others, unavailable to tour India in 1952–53; and had to settle for being something of a domestic hero with Essex. Never lost for a means of expressing himself, he also enjoyed two exceptional seasons with his new amateur football club, Walthamstow Avenue, after parting amicably with his old club, Leytonstone. He had kept, more or less, the extra stone throughout the 1951 cricket season, but this had little to do with the change of clubs that winter. The fact was that Leytonstone had found in Vic Groves a centre-forward of the highest class who was later to play for Arsenal with distinction. After a month in the Leytonstone reserves, Trevor decided to try his luck at finding a berth elsewhere.

Not much in the way of luck was needed. He describes how he found a niche with Walthamstow Avenue:

'I resigned from the club on the Monday, informed the press and went out to play canasta with my wife at the house of two close friends. We failed to complete one game, because the phone never stopped ringing with requests for me to join a whole series of clubs in the third division, the Southern League, and in various other leagues, both professional and amateur. It was all very flattering and was due mainly to my having become well known as a cricketer, in rather the same way that plenty of football clubs would want Ian Botham thirty years later.

'Although some of the offers received were very tempting financially, my objective was to find a club which was likely to do well and had a ground which I could reach in an hour by car. This narrowed my choice to virtually three clubs, because I had no intention of joining a Southern League side. On the Wednesday evening I saw the Barking and Walthamstow Avenue committees. I chose the latter because they had an immediate vacancy in their forward line and, having played against them so often, I knew they were an above-average, ambitious club. It proved to be an inspired choice, as we went on to capture the Amateur Cup that season. Although Walthamstow had a very distinguished record, that was something which had never happened to them before. In the following season, they experienced their best ever run in the FA Cup. I could not have chosen a better time to join the Avenue and I had two highly enjoyable and successful seasons with them.'

So his first season with Walthamstow found Bailey receiving an Amateur Cup-winner's medal in front of 100,000 people. It was one of those big occasions at which he excelled and consequently enjoyed to the hilt. The following season was to see his team, with him having

46

moved from inside-foward to the right wing, hold first-division Manchester United to a draw in the third round of the FA Cup, having beaten two professional clubs, Stockport County and Watford, on the way to those exalted heights.

Just how much all this took the edge from his cricket as opposed to keeping him fit for the summer game is open to question. What is less doubtful is that he made a considerable amount of money out of his time with Walthamstow Avenue, both through the fees he received through playing as an amateur and from the opportunities he gained for advertising products supposedly beneficial to attractive men who played cricket in summer and soccer in winter with a high measure of skill. Pictures of Trevor drinking Lucozade were to spring up everywhere.

Anyhow, cricket still provided his main source of income and, after the tour of Australia the previous winter, the 1951 season ranked as a disappointment. There was trouble at t'mill with Essex that season, which cannot have helped. R. F. T. Paterson, the Essex secretary, had grown disenchanted with doing nearly all the work while his assistant was, to all intents and purposes, being paid his salary for the more glamorous and enjoyable pursuit of playing cricket – and earning more money on the side as a result. So Bob Paterson tendered his resignation just prior to the AGM in 1951. This left Trevor still in the post of assistant secretary with Horace Clark, a dear, Pickwickian man, in the part of honorary secretary, a job he fulfilled with consummate skill while Trevor went about his lawful business on the field. But the upheaval must have been considerable and, with Trevor here, there and everywhere, Horace must have had his hands full.

Now is the time, probably, to get this amateur/professional thing into perspective. Trevor, as a street-wise and basic sort of fellow, was not one to rock the existing boat; but, as with cricket, he was one to take as much advantage of it as was reasonable in the circumstances. The life of a sportsman is hazardous. Injury can cut it short at any time.

The money coming into football and cricket was, in the early 1950s, almost entirely gathered through the turnstiles. Big sponsorship and TV deals were not at hand. Cricket was run as a game, not as a commercial enterprise, and you played it, even as professional, chiefly because you loved the way of life. As a rising star in this particular firmament, Trevor was instinctively led into the amateur ranks, and so he was not actually paid to play cricket; but he did not see why – given that, for amateurs, there was no tax-free benefit at the end of the rainbow – he should not take advantage of money-making opportunities as they came along. He was pragmatic enough to realise that his fame was to be transitory, and it was also his future.

As time went on, his writings, advertising, TV appearances and so on were not received with great warmth by some of those who had themselves enjoyed playing with all the advantages of being an amateur; sometimes picked by their counties because they came cheaper than the professionals, but now resentful of somebody who, despite his amateur status, made no bones about using his cricket for commercial ends. On the other side of the fence was the professional, who resented the special treatment afforded to amateurs as they made their way up and down the country, making money out of the game. Hypocrisy abounded in the search among the counties for amateur leaders. But Trevor was, above all, no hypocrite. His approach as a 'professional amateur' was to have a considerable influence on cricket at the highest levels but, to Trevor, the wider considerations were incidental.

So if the years 1951 and 1952 brought little in the way of advancement on the international scene, they did bring further fame and some fortune on the football field. Not that Bailey's performances for Essex were anything but of the highest quality by any standards. Still, in 1951, his two appearances for England against the South Africans, in the first and fourth Tests, found his bowling below its best. Having not been available, through leg trouble, for MCC's match against the tourists, he needed a good bowling performance in the first Test at Nottingham; although bowling well for forty-five overs in South Africa's first innings, he took none for 102. He also made few runs.

The emerging skills of Brian Statham as an opening bowler contributed towards Bailey not playing in the second and third Tests. Statham's dramatic and successful call to the England colours towards the end of the recent, ill-fated Australian tour had been successful, and he was now seen as Bedser's most likely new-ball partner. He did well, too, but a need to strengthen the batting brought about Bailey's recall for the fourth Test. Bailey rose to the occasion, making 95 runs out of England's 505, but strained his back while bowling in South Africa's record-breaking total of 538. This was to be his last innings in international cricket until the first Test in 1953.

England's loss was Essex's gain, however. In 1951, he scored more than 1,000 runs and took 91 wickets; in 1952 he made over 1,500 runs and, by taking 103 wickets, joined six other players – one of them his county colleague, Ray Smith – that season in completing the double.

But his finest hours were yet to come. The appointment of Len Hutton as England's first professional captain for the 1953 series against Australia had much to do with that.

3

At the Height of his Powers

1953

In *Cricket Heroes* John Woodcock wrote: 'In the 1950s, Trevor Bailey became a symbol of resistance. When England were in trouble on the cricket field, people would say: "It'll be all right, Bailey's still there." It was a reputation based more on intense application than great natural ability, and it had its origins at Lord's on 30th June 1953 when, with Willie Watson of Yorkshire, he shared in one of the greatest of all match-saving partnerships.'

Without wishing to take issue with one of our foremost cricket writers, and while acknowledging that what he says has more than an element of truth, there are two strands to his observation which bear closer scrutiny. First, Bailey's performance in the Lord's Test match of 1953 should have come as no surprise to those who had followed his career thus far. As recently as the MCC match against the Australians in May of that year, he had batted for three hours and forty minutes in MCC's second innings, having gone in at 55 for 4 and stayed until the end. Second, while Bailey's reputation as a batsman may well have been based on intense application, it would be wrong to infer that he did not possess great natural ability. It was just that he had worked it out. His role, as he saw it, and as so often was the case, was to be the bulwark in the middle of the order. This meant that he denied himself free rein for his natural talent – something which he possessed in abundance.

It is, however, an absolute truth that Bailey the cricketer had his most famous hour during the 1953 series against Australia and is best remembered for that innings of 71 when, in partnership with Willie Watson, he saved the match for England and, as it turned out,

50

enabled them to go on to win the Ashes for the first time for nineteen years.

The context in which that innings was played should be remembered. England's successes since the war had been few. Under Wally Hammond in 1946 in Australia they had been run ragged. Bradman's 1948 team had carried all before them. England's progress through Australia in 1950–51 had produced one victory in Test matches for them, but four for Australia. In 1948–49, England had won the series against South Africa, but in this country in 1949 all four matches against New Zealand had been drawn. And when, in 1950, West Indies not only achieved their first victory on English soil, but won the series by three matches to one, the English public had begun to search desperately for a fresh belief in English cricket. They needed new heroes. Especially, they needed to believe in England's ability to withstand the might of the Australians. Nineteen years was a long time. England had won a war and had displayed certain sterling qualities in doing so but, judged by the standards of those qualities, England had failed when confronted by the Aussies.

Always a wonderful game, cricket against Australia had taken on a deeper symbolism. Hassett's team in 1953 lacked one vital component. For the first time since 1926, the Australians had come to England without Donald George Bradman and, for all the fame of Hassett himself, Keith Miller, Ray Lindwall, Arthur Morris and Neil Harvey, there was a sense of high excitement among the public at the prospect of vulnerability in the Australian ranks. Hopes had been raised partly by a sweeping victory over the Indians in the 1952 series in England, partly by the fact that, for the first time, England were led by a professional captain who needed to win as much as everyone wanted him to. The feeling was that, under Len Hutton, England stood the best possible chance.

Not that early results gave any great cause for optimism in the England camp. The Australians made 542 in their only innings of a rain-affected match at Worcester, beat Leicestershire, Yorkshire and Surrey by an innings and, having tucked away Cambridge and Oxford Universities in similar fashion and had the better of a drawn match with MCC, they arrived for the first Test in Nottingham on 11th June unbeaten and fully in command. Any suspicions that the formidable Lindwall and Miller – names which tripped as easily off the tongue in those days as did Compton and Edrich or Hobbs and Sutcliffe – had lost some of their menace were dispelled. They were still rated as the best opening attack in the world, and Miller had shown early that he had lost none of his ability with the bat. He destroyed Yorkshire during the course of a partnership of 150 with Richie Benaud, a young lion who also bowled leg-breaks, after beginning the tour with an undefeated double century against Worcestershire.

Lindsay Hassett had been Bradman's vice-captain and soon gave evidence of his ability to mould together a team which contained four strangers to English conditions in the shape of Graeme Hole, Jim de Courcy, Alan Davidson and Benaud. Hassett's character, quiet but full of fun, breezy and chivalrous, was reflected in his team's attitude to the game and the way they played it. There was a lighter mood about them compared with the dour and analytical approach sought by Bradman, although this did not, at least in those early stages, appear to affect their ability to take the county games in their stride. So it was that, approaching the first Test match, they had fired the imagination of the English crowds as much with their style as with their obvious prowess.

If there were weaknesses in the 1953 Australians which had not been apparent when the team was selected, they lay in the inability of those picked as opening batsmen to settle down successfully in that role in England. Morris and Colin McDonald were the only two recognised openers and, with McDonald at a loss in a wet summer on uncovered pitches, Hassett, after experimenting with Hole, found himself going in first with Morris during the last four Test matches. Similarly, the discerning might have pointed to a noticeable imbalance in the Australian attack. Lindwall, Miller and Bill Johnston (left-arm fast-medium and slow spin) were a formidable enough trio, but three leg-spinners, Doug Ring, Jack Hill and Benaud, were hardly what the doctor would have prescribed for a summer in which rain played a major part. Two promising fast-bowling batsmen, Ron Archer and

Alan Davidson, were to fulfil their promise in later years, but the buzz was that England had a real chance of wresting back the Ashes.

But only the general flavour of all this was known before the first Test match at Nottingham. To be alive and keen on cricket in those days was a joy. Most other things of a day-to-day nature were submerged beneath talk of the matches against the Australians. As the series unfolded, it was clear that Fleet Street and radio and television had captured the mood of the moment. It is doubtful whether any series of Test matches, before or since, has captured such public attention. The crowds swarmed to them.

The public sense of anticipation was heightened by the way in which, throughout the series, the advantage swung from one side to the other, only to move back again. In this respect, the first Test set the trend. It also marked the zenith in the career of Alec Bedser who, during this match, passed the England Test record of 189 wickets held by S. F. Barnes, who was there to see it and, at eighty years of age, was one of the first to congratulate him. Bedser's 7 for 55 in the first innings and Bailey's 2 for 75 from forty-four overs saw Australia all out for 249; only Hassett with a century, Morris with 67 and Miller with 55 reached double figures. Australia had been 237 for 3 at one stage but, just as Englishmen up and down the country were thinking, 'Here we go again!' the first cracks in the Australian citadel that season began to show as their last 7 wickets melted away for the addition of only 12 runs.

England's gamble in going into the match with only four bowlers, including Bailey, had so far been successful beyond their wildest hopes. But a batting line-up which included Hutton, Don Kenyon, Reg Simpson, Compton, Tom Graveney, Peter May, and Bailey at No. 7, could muster no more than 144. So far from being in tatters, the Australian morale, boosted by a first-innings lead of more than 100 runs, was sky-high. Just one small cloud, no bigger than the proverbial man's fist, hovered on their horizon. Scarcely remarked at the time, but significant in what was to come, was an innings of 13 by Trevor Bailey. These runs occupied 100 minutes while Johnny Wardle was laying cheerfully about him at the other end. Bailey was already giving the Australian bowling a long, hard look.

53

Bedser's second haul of 7 wickets then left England needing 229 to win. A promising start, led by Hutton, was all that bad light and heavy rain throughout the rest of the match would allow. In spite of the disappointment felt at the lack of a positive result, the public's appetite had been well and truly whetted. In the England camp, elation was tempered with the knowledge that the balance of the team, with only four bowlers and one of them an all-rounder, had not been ideal, and that the exciting England effort had owed almost everything to one of them – Alec Bedser. On the credit side, however, had been the team spirit under Hutton which, according to Bailey, did much to overcome any lack of balance in the team and also, in some strange way, offset the disagreeable fact that it contained only three specialist close-to-the-wicket fielders.

'The result was curious,' says Bailey. 'Far from appearing unhappy in unaccustomed places, everyone managed to find a little extra ability, and some magnificent catches resulted. I particularly remember a running one by Simpson to send back Tallon which nobody expected Reg to reach, let alone hold. Then there was a spectacular catch by Graveney at backward short-leg to dismiss Harvey off a full-blooded hook. On paper, this was probably the worst fielding side to represent England in the whole series; yet, by some magic of team spirit or comradeship, it gave easily the best performance. This was the only time that England's fielding bore any comparison with the brilliance of Australia's.'

Whatever the feelings of Trevor Bailey and the general approval of the way the team at Nottingham had acquitted itself, three newcomers were drafted into the team to take on the Australians at Lord's for the second Test. Out went Simpson, May and Roy Tattersall; in came Watson, Statham and, much to the amazement of many, the then chairman of the Test selectors – Freddie Brown, he of the big heart, outstanding ability, simple philosophy and all of forty-two years. Brown's selection was indeed open to criticism. He himself did not wish to play, but Hutton and others persuaded him that this was a time for bold choices. Lord's was considered to be a venue worthy of special study. The slope was a factor. Leg-spin was in those days an essential ingredient of any side hoping to win and, by and large, it was felt that Freddie would be the man for that need if it arose.

Australia, like England, included a leg-spinner, but this time preferred Ring to Hill. Gil Langley was also preferred as wicket-keeper to Don Tallon. Whether or not this latter change had anything to do with Tallon's performance during the second Australian innings at Trent Bridge, history does not relate. It was not so much Tallon's wicket-keeping as the hardness of his hearing which resulted in the following contretemps.

As Tallon, so the story goes, was preparing to leave the dressing-room at the fall of Australia's sixth wicket, Hassett, in his quiet, close-mouthed way, is alleged to have instructed him in the following way: 'Give the light a go, Deafy.' One more appeal against the light was permitted the batsmen and, with Australia 6 wickets down for 81 and Bedser in full cry, Hassett wasn't all that anxious for play to continue. Arthur Morris was battling away at one end, and no one had made many at the other when Tallon arrived in the middle. As Morris advanced to meet him, the instructions from the dressing-room were relayed by Tallon in the following manner: 'The skipper says we've gotta give it a go.' Morris proceeded to do so to some effect and, as *Wisden* described, 'batted freely'. What *Wisden* does not describe was that, soon after Tallon's arrival at the crease, Morris was needlessly bowled round his legs having a swish at Tattersall, and it wasn't long before the Australian innings folded.

Anyhow, Langley was selected to take Tallon's place at Lord's in one of the most exciting Test matches seen even there – a match which, legend holds, saw more umbrella handles gnawed through than on any other occasion. The gates were closed half an hour before the start of the first day, and the crowds were packed cheek by jowl into the stands, many of them sitting in the aisles or standing in various parts of the ground.

At first, there was nothing for the rabid England supporter to write home about. Hassett had decided to seal a chink in the Australian armour by opening himself with Morris, having won the toss just as he had at Trent Bridge. The pitch was easy-paced, and Bailey remembers thinking at the time that some really outstanding fielding was needed to restore the balance between bat and ball. England's fielding was not good, however, and the only reward for some accurate bowling came when Morris was brilliantly stumped off Bedser from a ball which drifted down the leg side to Evans, standing up as he always did to Alec. It was a feat probably only Jack Russell of present-day cricketers could hope to accomplish.

Slowly but surely during the course of the afternoon, Australia established through Hassett and Harvey what appeared to be a firm grip on the game. At tea, they were 180 for one wicket. But England were far from done with. Harvey was out for 59 playing a shot which Bailey thought was more suitable to a hard wicket in Australia than to Lord's on that day in June, and Hassett, having completed his second century of the summer, made what turned out to be a crucial error when he retired from the field, suffering from cramp. England were amazed that someone batting so assuredly did not continue with a runner. For suddenly Australia were vulnerable at both ends, and intelligent bowling, by Wardle in particular, meant that England were able to take five wickets for 263 by the close. If Hassett had not left the field when he did, Bailey believes that England's position might have been almost beyond repair.

As it was, despite a brilliant 76 by Alan Davidson, England were by no means disheartened by the Australian first-innings total of 346. They took the last five Australian wickets on the second day, including that of Hassett, for 83 on a true pitch. It is true to say that everyone on the England team, including their captain, would have felt even better had they held on to several chances that went down. Hutton himself missed three of them, and Davidson should have been out twice early in his innings.

By the end of the second day, the balance of power was even. As if to make up for his lapses in the field, Hutton was masterly in the way he dealt with his old adversaries, Lindwall and Miller. The crowd were treated to English batting at its best against some of the best bowling in the world. After Kenyon had fallen early on, Graveney helped Hutton to put on 168, equalling the previous highest second-wicket stand for

England against Australia since the war. It was a sight the vast crowd had been waiting to see. There was elation in the streets of St John's Wood when play came to a close with the England score standing at 177 for one wicket, and the prospect of many more runs lying just around the corner.

So England began that third day of the five-day match just 170 runs behind with nine wickets in hand, and with Hutton and Graveney having established such dominance the evening before that the thoughts of all those who packed Lord's on the Saturday morning were on a huge first-innings lead. The Saturday of the Lord's Test when England play Australia is always *the* big occasion in the cricketing calendar. Now you could hardly breathe, so intense was the atmosphere of anticipation.

It was as if the crowd let out its collective breath in one great surge. With no addition to the England score, Graveney was out, his middle and off stumps leaning drunkenly after he had played over a yorker from Lindwall. The sense of anti-climax was all the more potent for the reason that everyone was gearing themselves for a new-ball onslaught from Lindwall and Miller; what they had not anticipated was a wicket from a loosener with the old one. But the battle with the new ball was to live up to the highest expectations. It was won by Hutton and Compton but, in stretching the skill and nerve of these two to near breaking point, Lindwall, ably supported by Miller, bowled magnificently. The hundred partnership, and Hutton's 2,000 runs against Australia, were milestones that flicked by before Hutton's innings ended. At lunch, England were 59 behind with seven wickets left. They lunched well in the Tavern that day: the talk was all about Hutton's wonderful 145 and England's strong position.

But that was an end to England's rejoicing. In under two hours, they lost their last seven wickets for 93 runs. Bailey contributed only two of these. He stuck around while 41 runs were added for the loss of three more wickets before departing to Miller's slower ball, straining, as he describes it, to do more than simply hit the fielders with mistimed drives. It was one more such effort that presented Miller with an easy return catch.

Largely through the efforts of Morris and Miller in the second innings – Miller's century further underlined his liking for Lord's, which he had by now adopted as his own – Australia moved almost out of sight. The crowd loved Miller. But none of this furthered England's cause and, above all, that was what the crowd wanted. Spirits were low as Australia piled on the runs, especially when Lindwall, batting at No. 9, drove his way to 50 in forty-five minutes. Finally, some seventy minutes before the end of the fourth day's play, Australia were all out, leaving England to score 343 to win. This was a tall order on a wearing pitch, but there had been so many twists and turns of fortune in this match that anything seemed possible as Hutton and Kenyon made their way to the wicket to see out the last hour, gather a few runs, provide a platform for the morrow. For the Australians, larking around and tossing the ball to each other as they made their way to the middle, it was an opportunity to have an all-out burst at the opposition; nothing to lose, everything to gain. Bailey was already padding up as Hutton prepared to receive Lindwall's first ball. It had been decided that, should a wicket fall at 6 o'clock or after, he would go in as nightwatchman, rather than risk a specialised batsman.

It was a decision which need not have been taken. From 6 p.m. onwards, Bailey was waiting to bat in his rightful position of fourth wicket down. England, already demoralised by Lindwall's onslaught with the bat, had him to thank for their hopeless position at the end of the day. For, inside half an hour, they had lost 3 wickets for 12 runs. Kenyon completed an unhappy match by driving Lindwall to Hassett at mid-on, and then Hutton was taken low down in the slips by Hole from a perfectly-pitched out-swinger, Lindwall's stock-in-trade, a ball which few batsmen would have managed to touch. At the other end, Johnston induced Graveney to snick, Langley took the best, most important diving catch of his career – or so it seemed at the time – and Compton and Watson were left to struggle for dear life as gloom descended.

Bailey, next man in, swears he remained composed throughout a chapter of near misses as Watson sought to keep Ring at bay in those final overs before the close. The leg-spinner, pitching into the rough outside the left-hander's off stump, caused Watson to grope un-certainly; and while Compton, the incomparable, played easily enough, Watson was all edges. The last over of the day saw him dropped, off Ring, at short-leg.

So uncertain had been England's batting, so ascendant had been the Australians throughout that Monday in late June, that everyone in England was resigned to Australia going one up in the series. The weather forecast was no help; no hint of face-saving rain. Yet, despite the weather, the ground was only half-full. It was a marked contrast to the four previous days when, without exception, paying customers had had to be turned away.

In these days of four-star hotels where players can rightly relax in comparative comfort, it is quaintly odd to think of one of England's batsmen-in-waiting taking the train to Westcliff-on-Sea at the close of play. But that is what Trevor Bailey did. Travelling to London on the morning of the final day on the smoky route to Liverpool Street, he read the papers. From Swanton in the *Telegraph* to Rostron in the *Express*, the writers had reflected public opinion in, politely or otherwise, writing England off.

Denis Compton, hero of many Tests, but now hampered by an arthritic knee, was seen as a possible trump card in England's hand. He had played well overnight – and in England's first innings – was patently in form, and was still capable of making a big score, even on a wearing pitch. But the rest had been largely discounted. It was a reasonable view, coming as it did from gut-feeling and a grave sense of disappointment at England's performance in the ebbing moments of Monday evening. Bailey himself remembered the quiet despair on the face of England's captain, Len Hutton, as he unbuckled his pads, sick in the realisation that to lose the Lord's Test match would be to fail to recapture the Ashes, the aim towards which he had planned and worked ever since he had first led the team against India. Lose here, and England, lacking confidence and up against an Australian team positively imbued with it, would have to win two of the remaining three.

Compton took up on the Tuesday just where he had left off, middling everything, settling in comfortably with Watson. The morning had been eaten into by an hour and a half when the maestro received a near unplayable shooter from Bill Johnston, bowling his left-arm fast-medium stuff; it caught Compton just above the ankle, back on his stumps and bang in front. Nearly five hours remained, and England were now 73 for 4 wickets.

Bailey was frankly pessimistic about England's chances of saving the match. He was, though, he says, 'narked' at the way England were being consigned to fail quite so readily. It was with a firm feeling of 'it's not all over until the fat lady sings' that he approached the wicket. His one aim was to stay there as long as he could.

By now, he had developed to the full various mannerisms which, if not calculated, certainly served to annoy the Aussies, none more so than Keith Miller, the swashbuckling Australian all-rounder, glamour and spontaneity his trade marks. There was an infuriating 'cool' about Bailey which bordered on disdain. His head thrown back as he made his way to the wicket; not a crinkly hair out of place; a confidence bordering on the overripe; all the hallmarks of a bloody nuisance. There was the loud, rather self-satisfied way he called for or refused a run, too certain by far, arrogant almost. Bailey was to learn, if only subsequently, that these traits were among his best assets when dealing with the Australians and, indeed, with fast bowlers of all nationalities. Irritated opponents were seldom able to give of their absolute best and, one way or another, Trevor managed to irritate them all.

The Australian team of 1953 had as yet no real concept of all this. His batting in the Test matches of the Freddie Brown tour had brought him an average of only 8 runs an innings. He had, it is true, batted for nearly four hours against them while making 64 not out in the MCC match at Lord's, but then Lindwall had been unable to bowl against him.

Always a realist, Bailey knew that survival on this pitch would be something of a miracle. Two leg-spinners in Ring and Benaud, and Bill Johnston in his slower, spinning role, were there to take advantage of the considerable turn which the wicket now allowed. Nor far away was the second new ball. Lindwall and Miller looked eager. Backing them up was the fast left-arm of Alan Davidson.

Willie Watson had settled down after an edgy, uncertain start, but the worn patches outside his off stump were causing him trouble against the leg-spinners. As Bailey quietly played himself in for half an hour, it occurred to both of them that his chances of survival against the leg-spinners were the better for his being a right-hander. Consequently, he took as much of Ring and Benaud as he could without, he says, 'making it look too obvious'.

Lunch came with the two of them still not looking absolutely secure, but with Watson past 50 and Bailey just into double figures. It is a measure of Trevor's imperturbability that he saw no reason to change his eating habits at this crucial moment. While Watson drank milk, Trevor tucked into a three-course meal. Sitting in the dressing-room quiet and alone as the rest of the team went into the Lord's dining-room, they discussed what lay ahead. They agreed that the supreme test would come midway through the afternoon, when the new ball became due. They also knew that facing the leg-spin of Ring and Benaud was not going to be a picnic, especially for Watson, and resolved to take no liberties with either while not allowing the bad ball to go unpunished. But, to their relief, Hassett saw things differently.

Trevor says he was amazed when Bill Johnston and Alan Davidson took the ball after lunch. He and Watson had a healthy fear of leg-spin on this pitch, second only to the forthcoming new ball in the hands of Lindwall and Miller. Now they were being given the chance to get accustomed to pace with the old ball before facing the onslaught with the new. Hassett brought back Benaud after a while; but by then the damage had been done. The dress rehearsal for the pace of Lindwall and Miller had gone well. The two were playing confidently when, just before 3 p.m., Lindwall and Miller flexed their muscles in preparation for the all-out thrust upon which the fate of this match, and possibly the destination of the Ashes, seemed bound to hinge.

As the white and yellow discs denoting that the new ball was due went up on the score-boards, T. E. Bailey felt a sense of exhilaration. It was as if he had lived his life for this moment. He says that Willie Watson and he exchanged a glance which spoke volumes. This was it. This was what it was all about. All round the ground the silent crowd leaned in.

The next forty minutes were almost unbearably tense. Only 12 runs

61

were scored in that period. Bailey's forward defensive – the left hand slid round the grip as the bowler bowled so that the front of the hand went to the rear and the bat was finely angled when it met the ball – brought him trouble of a physical kind. Three times he was hit painfully on the hand, dropped his bat, wrung his hand, carried on. Hatless (and certainly helmetless), the two of them got behind every ball. Frequently they were forced to duck or sway inside the bouncer; Miller's steeply rising, Lindwall's with his low, slinging action skimming through wickedly at chest- or throat-height. Purely defensive strokes brought applause from a crowd whose pent-up feelings needed some release. It was war to the knife. And Bailey, in his element, relished every moment.

Watson, too, played impeccably. 'As a Lancashire man I looves yer, Willie,' rang out from the Mound Stand, from a crowd absorbed in the moment, visibly increasing as the day wore on, and men in their offices made an excuse and left. This tribute to the left-handed Yorkshireman eased the tension briefly; the tea interval came as a great relief. Still people hardly dared talk of the match being saved. But the *possibility* was in the air. The buzz around the ground was animated, excited. There were just over two hours of play remaining. England went to tea at 183 for 4.

As they did so, Freddie Brown, immovable while play was in progress, heaved his considerable bulk off his seat. The superstition exists in cricket that you don't move during an important stand, and wild horses wouldn't have moved F. R. Brown that afternoon. When play resumed, Brown returned at once to his place on the players' balcony.

He was there for even longer than he dared hope. On and on went Watson and Bailey. Watson completed his century, sweeping Ring to the square-leg boundary but, with the game almost safe, with the old Lord's clock tower reading 10 minutes to 6, Watson's innings, which had lasted five and three-quarter hours, came to an end. A googly from Ring saw him taken at first slip. The applause for Watson was heartfelt, the hearts of those applauding somewhere near their boots as Freddie Brown advanced to do battle. Only thirty-five minutes remained until the end of this epic Test match, yet nobody watching would have dared to say that England were safe. Bailey was still there, and there were only 5 wickets down. But so capricious had been the gods of cricket, so sudden the changes of fortune throughout, that nobody quite believed that they did not have one last, wicked throw up their sleeves.

When Hassett failed to bring back Lindwall to confront Brown, who had been sitting in the dark of the pavilion all day and would have found Lindwall's pace a severe trial, he gave England the best chance of making certain. Even when Bailey played a slash at Ring, was caught at cover, threw back his head in anguish and departed, there was really scant chance of Australia succeeding with only twenty-five minutes left. Brown met the spinners by driving them ferociously; more time was wasted as the ball was retrieved. When he was out, in the last over, it was still technically possible for Australia to win. Every ball of the four remaining, played by Wardle, was met with the middle of the bat. Even so, it was difficult to believe that the match had been saved, some time before it all sank in.

The second Test against Australia at the game's headquarters was to prove a turning-point in Trevor Bailey's career. Already recognised as an all-round player of talent, he was now on the way to becoming, in the eyes of the British public, one of cricket's immortals. It had all happened in the right place at the right time. And it had happened when everyone had been resigned to it not happening. Bailey's determination and his gift for sheer bloody-minded resistance were now confirmed in his own mind as the best means by which to further the interests of England, and to further his own career. His bowling action already modified, his search towards finding a successful *modus operandi* for his batting was at an end. Give him a bat, or a ball, or place him anywhere in the field, and he would perform. Mr Reliable he had become; it was now his trademark.

There were to be times when he could be reasonably accused of making a drama out of a crisis. 'If there is no crisis, Trevor will create one,' was later to be the cry of his critics. There were to be times when his batting seemed insufferably dull for the sake of it, and the odd innings, by virtue of its tempo, was said to serve the opposition better

England v Australia. Second Test at Lord's. June 25, 26, 27, 28, 29, 30 1953

Australia

A. L. Hassett c Bailey b Bedser	104	— c Evans b Statham	3
A. R. Morris st Evans b Bedser	30	— c Statham b Compton	89
R. N. Harvey lbw b Bedser	59	— b Bedser	21
K. R. Miller b Wardle	25	— b Wardle	109
G. B. Hole c Compton b Wardle	13	— lbw b Brown	47
R. Benaud lbw b Wardle	0	— c Graveney b Bedser	5
A. K. Davidson c Statham b Bedser	76	— c and b Brown	15
D. Ring lbw b Wardle	18	— lbw b Brown	7
R. R. Lindwall b Statham	9	— b Bedser	50
G. R. Langley c Watson b Bedser	1	— b Brown	9
W. A. Johnston not out	3	— not out	0
B 4, 1-b 4	8	B 8, 1-b 5	13

1/65 2/190 3/225 4/229 5/240 6/280   346   1/3 2/168 3/227 4/235   368
7/291 8/330 9/331   5/248 6/296 7/305 8/308 9/362

England

L. Hutton c Hole b Johnston	145	— c Hole b Lindwall	5
D. Kenyon c Davidson b Lindwall	3	— c Hassett b Lindwall	2
T. W. Graveney b Lindwall	78	— c Langley b Johnston	2
D. C. S. Compton c Hole b Benaud	57	— lbw b Johnston	33
W. Watson st Langley b Johnston	4	— c Hole b Ring	109
T. E. Bailey c and b Miller	2	— c Benaud b Ring	71
F. R. Brown c Langley b Lindwall	22	— c Hole b Benaud	28
T. G. Evans b Lindwall	0	— not out	11
J. H. Wardle b Davidson	23	— not out	0
A. V. Bedser b Lindwall	1		
J. B. Statham not out	17		
B 11, 1-b 1, w 1, n-b 7	20	B 7, 1-b 6, w 2, n-b 6	21

1/9 2/177 3/279 4/291 5/301 6/328   372   1/6 2/10 3/12   (7 wkts.)   282
7/328 8/332 9/341   4/73 5/236 6/246 7/282

England Bowling

	O.	M.	R.	W.		O.	M.	R.	W.
Bedser	42.4	8	105	5	....	31.5	8	77	3
Statham	28	7	48	1	....	15	3	40	1
Brown	25	7	53	0	....	27	4	82	4
Bailey	16	2	55	0	....	10	4	24	0
Wardle	29	8	77	4	....	46	18	111	1
Compton						3	0	21	1

Australia Bowling

	O.	M.	R.	W.		O.	M.	R.	W.
Lindwall	23	4	66	5	....	19	3	26	2
Miller	25	6	57	1	....	17	8	17	0
Johnston	35	11	91	2	....	29	10	70	2
Ring	14	2	43	0	....	29	5	84	2
Benaud	19	4	70	1	....	17	6	51	1
Davidson	10.5	2	25	1	....	14	5	130	
Hole						1	1	0	0

Umpires: F. S. Lee and H. G. Baldwin.

64

than it benefited his own team. But the die was finally cast in June 1953, and he was just what Len Hutton had cried out for since he had been appointed captain of England. Indeed, England, and Len Hutton in particular, were to have cause to be even more grateful to him before the series was done. And Len was to listen more to Bailey than to anyone if it came to discussion or advice on the tactical means whereby the Aussies could be defeated.

It is a remarkable fact that – possibly because he entered the fray in similar fashion throughout his Test career – Bailey's part in the stand is universally more easily remembered than Willie Watson's. Watson batted longer, scored his runs faster, looked in many ways the more accomplished player. He was also a graceful player, which perhaps disguised an equally indomitable spirit. Trevor's taste for mild histrionics possibly helped him here, imprinted him indelibly on the memory.

The magnitude of their achievement at Lord's was given the most extraordinary coverage by the press. Neville Cardus, for example, on the morning after the match, led the front page of the *Manchester Guardian* (as it was then) under the headline 'Miracle of Faith at Lord's'. Bailey's name was on everyone's lips, before everyone's eyes.

From Lord's, where nearly £58,000 in gate money had been taken – a record at the time for any cricket match – and nearly 140,000 people had watched the contest, the series moved on to Manchester. It was a rain-bedevilled occasion, which proved just as well for England. Having left out Statham and gone into the match with four bowlers, they were further handicapped by an injury to Laker. They very nearly did succeed in bowling out Australia inside an hour on the last day on a wet wicket, but then there was no chance of a result, even had they done so.

It was in the fourth Test that Bailey again saved England. The circumstances were less spectacular, but the prospects of defeat were just as real as they had been at Lord's. This time Leeds was the venue, and in Yorkshire there was an audience tuned to appreciate this southerner who gave nowt away and refused to admit defeat. They had plenty of time to appreciate him.

To start with, he damaged a knee. He was in good company: Simpson was struck on the point of the elbow by Lindwall; Watson damaged an ankle; and Laker pulled a muscle. Once England had gone into the match with four bowlers and two of them were handicapped, they were bound to be up against it. Bailey bowled off a short run in the first Australian innings and Laker, despite his injury, hobbled on. Bailey took 3 good wickets off an eight-pace run.

Australia's lead of 99 at the half-way mark and with three days left, in dubious weather and on an uncovered pitch, was a valuable advantage. This match, and so the Ashes too, would almost certainly have been lost had not Bailey, now well in the groove against the Australian attack, contrived to drop anchor for four hours and twenty minutes for 38 match-saving runs. Denis Compton's right hand had become so swollen after a painful blow that he could hardly hold his bat and was forced to retire for a while; and with England five wickets down with a lead of only 72, Bailey's innings was absolutely invaluable.

It was dull but resolute batting, appreciated by all except the Australians, as Lindwall and Miller sent down a barrage of bouncers and Hassett wished he had an orthodox spinner to call upon. Bailey had great help from the Surrey members of the tail. Laker, Bedser and Lock stayed with him and stretched England's second innings, played on and off for three days over nine hours and forty minutes, to within just over two hours of the finish. Australia then needed 177 runs to win.

Hutton thought England could win. Bailey certainly thought Australia would have their backs to the wall and that they could be in all kinds of trouble. With memories of the Australian second-innings débâcle at Old Trafford firmly in mind, the whole England team moved confidently out to the middle. For their part, the Australians were thinking not so much of winnings as of avoiding ever again looking such complete mugs as they had been made to look on the other side of the Pennines in not dissimilar circumstances.

As it happened, everyone was wrong. Hutton opened with Bedser, whose first-innings 6 for 95 was still firmly in mind, and the slow left-arm of Lock. Both bowled to attacking fields, and from the start runs came freely. Neither Bedser nor Lock was at his best, and Lock was positively wayward, suffering at the hands of the left-handed Morris to the tune of 14 off his first over. It was a landslip that was to become an avalanche. Lock was meat and drink to the left-handers: Morris first, then Harvey, picked off the gaps in the field. Although Hassett fell to Lock and, having scorched to 38, Morris was stumped off Laker when he replaced his Surrey spin-twin, Harvey and Graeme Hole brought up the 100 inside an hour. By comparison with this, the scoring of the 66 runs needed for victory in the forty-five minutes after Harvey was lbw to Bedser, seemed a cake-walk.

It was now that Trevor Bailey took over. It was clear that Hutton was nonplussed by the turn of events. Bailey had been on the field all day, batting or fielding, but as yet he had not bowled. During the course of the huddle which formed after Harvey lost his wicket, Trevor took Len on one side. What followed was a thoroughly professional plea from a very professionally-minded amateur, supported by Bill Edrich, another amateur and a veteran of more than thirty Tests. 'We've got to slow down the over rate', said Bailey. 'That means using me with Alec. I'll bowl off my long run. And I want six men on the leg side.' Hutton agreed. Anything to avoid throwing the match and the Ashes away. The question was whether the door had already been allowed to swing too far open.

From twenty-one overs, bowled in seventy minutes, 111 runs had been scored. When Bailey came on to bowl, the over rate had been well above seventeen an hour. In the final forty-five minutes, Bailey and Bedser bowled twelve overs: statistically, not that much slower, but the way in which Bailey bowled meant that runs dried up at his end, and there was precious little time wasted in chasing the ball to the boundary. In fact, the time taken between deliveries must have seemed like ages to the Australians.

Legislation later took over to prevent negative leg-side tactics such as Bailey applied that day. But it was extremely effective, though magisterially frowned upon by the pundits of the time. When the rampant Graeme Hole was beautifully caught on the square-leg boundary by Graveney, off Bailey, and the pinpoint accuracy of Bailey's bowling gave the other batsmen no room for manoeuvre as they were tucked up round the leg stump, the danger to England receded. Only 36 runs came from the last twelve overs. In six of these overs, Bailey conceded only 9 runs.

It is, of course, rare in a modern Test match that more than fourteen overs an hour are bowled, whatever the circumstances, however fresh the bowler. Indeed, twelve overs is more the norm: different times, different actions, different customs. But, across a wide range of opinion in 1953, Bailey's ploy was considered as close as you could get to bending the spirit of the game without actually breaking it. But deliberate time-wasting was not a charge that could be levelled – not that anybody showed any inclination to do so. Yet it is said that his opponents never forgave Bailey for stringing out one over to seven minutes.

By now, the Australians were getting heartily sick of this bloke who played the game in a way they understood, envied even, but had fast become a 'pain in the ass' in every way. 'If he wasn't catching you or bowling you he was standing in your way like a barn door,' said one. Bailey had also in those last defiant overs ensured that the final Test at the Oval held out the prospect of the Ashes to both teams.

It was agreed that the time allowed for this Test should be six days. This was not, in any way, a concession to Bailey's scoring rate or, indeed, his over rate, which was generally well up with the rest of his kind. The extension was geared towards obtaining a definite result. But six days were not needed.

Hutton had managed to lose the toss in every previous Test match, and now at the Oval he managed to do so again. The toss matters less these days than it did then. Rarely, very rarely, did you put the opposition in during the time of uncovered wickets. The chance of batting on a dry, well-prepared surface was invariably taken. Rain could render any surface tricky for batting: better take the chance to bat first whenever you could; occupy the crease. With all this in mind, the England dressing-room was a gloomy place when the news of Hutton's loss was relayed, although the feeling was one of resignation at the trick played by the fates rather than dejection. What they did not know then, but what in hindsight was to become a salient fact, was that losing the toss was the most potent element in England's eventual victory. It had everything to do with the weather and uncovered pitches.

Trevor Bailey felt that, almost for the first time in the series, England had a well-balanced attack. In the first Test, England had had only four bowlers, with Bedser and himself to use the new ball. Lord's had been better: Bedser and Statham had opened the bowling, with Bailey as third seamer and all-rounder. The third Test had seen England get away with it again, despite Statham's absence through injury and a reversion to a four-man attack. Then Fred Trueman had been left out at Headingley, despite having been called up to replace Statham in the England twelve. Injury had always played some part in the final make-up of the teams, but so too had Hutton's wariness about the as yet immature Trueman, and the tactical consideration surrounding each Test match.

Now at the Oval, however, England had a balanced attack: Bedser, Trueman, Bailey, Laker and Lock. Furthermore, here was a chastened yet belligerent Trueman, anxious to prove himself as 't' finesty bloody fast bowler who ever drew breath'. In the wilderness throughout the season, unable to reproduce his form of the previous summer when he had routed the Indians, he was raring to go. The Australians had not seen Trueman before. Furthermore, the Oval was renowned for helping spin at an early stage. Laker and Lock had both had triumphant seasons there, and the fact that the Australians picked only one spinner for this match was always, to Bailey's mind, a great potential source of aid to England. Still, losing the toss . . . yet again. As England trooped out to field, all the advantages seemed to have been nullified.

But that first day of the final Test conspired in England's favour. Short bursts of rain served to enliven the pitch just as it appeared to have returned to its early placidity. Throughout the day, cloud cover helped the ball to swing. Trevor says he had difficulty in controlling the ball during his first spell, so much was the ball swinging; but it helped him claim the notable scalp of Miller, unusually padding up to a ball that swung late into him. And then there was Trueman. Despite a sound half-century by Hassett and solid innings by Harvey and Hole,

Australia had rarely been on top: Trueman's speed, his long run and his bouncer electrified the crowd and cost Australia four wickets. Bedser's 3 wickets included that of Arthur Morris for the eighteenth time in twenty Tests and brought him a record in Australia/England series of 39 wickets. But Bailey expresses disappointment with the total achieved by Australia that day. Several vital catches were dropped. He himself was belaboured by Alan Davidson, the burly left-hander, after having him put down at slip. A stand between Davidson and Lindwall developed, Lindwall shared another with Langley and, from 160 for 7, Australia took their score to 275, Lindwall making 62 of them.

Still, it was better than England could have expected when they lost the toss. At least the wicket was still reasonably good, and Australia had nobody really able to take advantage when it took more spin. Bailey remembers the only two Australian overs bowled that day as two of the fastest he has seen: Lindwall and Miller really let Hutton and Edrich have it. One ball from Lindwall caused Hutton to play an improvised defensive shot to prevent the ball drilling a hole in him; and his cap, which fell off at the same time, just missed his wicket. Survival was achieved by a coat of varnish.

It is a reminder of those days, and of the attitudes prevailing, that the next day, Sunday, should have seen Trevor opening a new pavilion in Southend and, having been billed to play, batting for one of the local clubs. Having bowled fourteen overs on the Saturday of the Test, he declined to do so here.

On Monday, the second day of the Test, thousands were locked out of the Oval. The scent of an England victory was in the air. Yet, even with their unbalanced attack, the day turned out to be very much the Australians'. Significantly, not Miller, not Lindwall – well as both of them bowled – proved to be their most effective weapon. Instead, it was the dual-purpose Bill Johnston who caused most problems. Shortening his run, spinning and cutting the ball from leg, and bowling with uncanny accuracy, it was Johnston who accounted for Hutton and the young Peter May after they had contributed a century stand and Hutton had made 82. Lindwall, a wonderful bowler on any surface, also made inroads, but the tell-tale signs were beginning to appear; the pitch was already favouring spin. Graeme Hole, a very occasional bowler, was brought on and caused the out-of-form Graveney and Compton trouble. Interestingly, Bailey lays part of the blame for this on Hole's high trajectory and the lack of sight-screens at the Vauxhall Road end (more shades of the past). Whatever the reasons, England quickly lost the advantage given by Hutton and May. When May was out, England were 137 for 2. At tea, they were 165 for 3 after four hours' batting. When Bailey came to the wicket, England had scored 167 for 4; it quickly became 170 for 5 when Graveney was out, just after Lindwall had taken the second new ball.

Bailey's fabulous season had thus far depended upon his ability to stick around in the most trying of circumstances, and little else. It was something at which he had become adept. Little else was expected of him. It was now that he showed the extent of his confidence. He took command as if assured of his destiny.

At first, 'taking command' in the Bailey fashion meant securing one end while Godfrey Evans took Lindwall and Miller, and the new ball, to task at the other. The Australians had by now grown used to the pendulum of Bailey's forward and backward defensive strokes. But Evans, chancing his arm and enjoying the odd slice of outrageous luck was something for which they had not bargained. Evans made 28 of the 40 runs these two added for the sixth wicket. It had been Bailey in familiar mode, nor did he find the opportunity for much more than solid defence as England inched their way to 235 for 7 by the close. Trevor was undefeated with 35 by then, however, and had so far forgotten himself as to take 11 off one over from Johnston.

Tony Lock had stayed with Bailey for forty minutes on Monday evening and, when the two of them resumed on Tuesday morning, England were 40 runs behind Australia on the first innings with not a lot in the way of proven batting to come. It was not long before the next man – Trueman – joined Bailey. Bailey was surprised at Fred's elevation in the order. At 237 for 8 he expected to see Alec Bedser, a better batsman against fast bowling than Trueman was ever likely to be, coming to the wicket. In the event, Trueman played a noble part, staying while 25 were added.

In those days the psychological advantage of a first-innings lead seems to have been immense. When Bailey, with Bedser, eased England in front, the cheer could be heard throughout Kennington. The two put on 44 for the last wicket; England gained a first-innings lead of 31 runs; and Bailey, after batting for three and three-quarter hours for his 64 – an innings which saw him give no chance and during which he hit seven fours – had provided the platform from which a real challenge could be launched. The game was there for the taking.

Bailey did not bat or bowl again in the match. Yet his was a major part in the Test which returned the Ashes to England. By acting both as the core of resistance and as the senior partner when joined by the tail-enders he had not only given England the lead, small as it was; but he had kept a wearing wicket occupied long enough by England to ensure that Australia would be facing Laker and Lock on a pitch ideal for the spinners' purposes. Mainly through Ron Archer, who hit out at anything even remotely pitched up and made 49, Australia managed 162 in their second innings. It never looked enough. These were sentimental days, and the public were delighted that the Middlesex twins, Compton and Edrich, were in at the end when the winning runs were made and England had won by 8 wickets. But everyone knew that, without Bailey, the series could never have been England's.

As a postscript, almost, Bailey captained the Gentleman of England against the Australians. It was a match which the Gentlemen might conceivably have won had they possessed more than one spinner. As it was, they had the better of the first two days, and there was praise for Bailey's leadership.

The year 1953 was, without doubt, the pinnacle of Bailey's career. His performances touched a chord to which Englishmen everywhere responded. He captained two representative teams against the tourists. At the end of it all, he was appointed vice-captain to Len Hutton in the team to tour the West Indies. A favourite son of Essex was now a favourite – and favoured – son of the public; and of the highest circles of English cricket.

He summed it up later in words which gave an idea of his matter-of-fact approach, his penchant for weighing up carefully every aspect of the subject – and his prose style: 'It was a wonderful series to play in,' he wrote. 'I shall always treasure the memory of my part in the contest, and I am most grateful for the way my efforts were received. It is rare to earn praise for batting and bowling that were neither spectacular nor particularly impressive statistically.'

A touch of false modesty? Possibly. But he had earned the right.

4

Vice-captain to Hutton

1953–54

In so far as cricketers in the public eye can mirror the hopes and aspirations of the young of their time, the young cricketer of the 1950s saw in Trevor Bailey a model of everything he wanted to be. Bailey was the chap who was always in the picture: batting, bowling, and fielding. In the days when heroes of the Resistance were still remembered, he had become a hero of resistance – particularly against those time-honoured enemies, the Australians.

At the age of twenty-nine, Bailey was at the height of his powers. He knew exactly where he was going. His batting at Test-match level, although set in the defensive mode which had already earned him the soubriquet of 'Barnacle', among others, especially when the Australians were doing the calling, had earned the respect of all who played against him. His bowling had settled into the speed and rhythm best suited to admirable control, maximum late movement through the air, and the ability to sustain long spells of good wickets, constantly working at the weaknesses of opposing batsmen. He studied them and he knew them well. As a fielder, close to the wicket, he brought off those catches you like to dream about, finishing with the ball clutched in his very fingertips, spreadeagled on the turf, the batsman wearing that baffled look which seemed to say: 'How on earth did he catch that? He had no right to do that. It was a perfectly well-played shot.'

Bailey had, in those days of the early 1950s, and especially in 1953, all the hallmarks of a hero from the *Boys Own Paper*. Television had not by then spoiled the imagination. There was little probing by the camera to expose frailties in the character, no lingering on the face of disappointment or disgust at the way a decision had gone. In any case, people still behaved themselves in public. So the heroic concept was largely intact; and Bailey – because he was, if somewhat haughtily, good-looking, because he batted and bowled as if his life and the lives of others depended on it – had for young and old alike some of the qualities they admired.

Others were near the end of their careers. Len Hutton, the first professional to captain England; Denis Compton, cavalier, devil-may-care, was nursing a ghastly arthritic knee which stifled his erstwhile carefree movement; and Bill Edrich, gritty, gutsy, but past his best. But Godfrey Evans was a nonpareil wicket-keeper. Then there were the up-and-coming batsmen, tried, tested, but not yet absolutely proven: Tom Graveney, Peter May and Colin Cowdrey. And the still fledgling bowlers, snapping at the heels of the incomparable Alec Bedser: Trueman, Frank Tyson, Statham, a whiff of Peter Loader. Finally, the trove was rich in spin: Laker, Lock, Wardle, Bob Appleyard.

Len Hutton, Bailey's captain during his most productive period, yielded to nobody in his admiration of the young man's qualities. It was Hutton who pressed Bailey into service as an opening batsman, Hutton who doubtless had a hand in making him a possible heir-apparent by taking Bailey as his vice-captain to West Indies. It was Hutton who knew a sharp, cool, tactical cricket brain when he saw one, and who leaned, as a professional, upon an amateur every bit as 'professional' as he was. Yet Len's advocacy and Trevor's ability in terms of captaincy were destined never to bear fruit at England level: the hierarchy at Lord's were not ready for someone who combined such self-composure on the field with professional mien and, at the same time, possessed the relative freedom of thought and action, open in those days in its entirety only to the amateur. The mind's eye, looking through the window of the committee-room at Lord's, may well have been wary of a Trevor Bailey. As a potential leader he may have been touched with a faint shadow of Douglas Jardine, a kind of stop-at-nothing attitude if it meant winning: Len Hutton without the professional's deference.

In any case, the opportunity was to arise to write off Bailey as a possible England captain, and then along came May – Peter, that is. It was sad in many ways that the chance of having someone as captain who would be on the field virtually throughout all five days of a Test match, whether batting, bowling or fielding, could not have been provided as the supreme test for Bailey. Ian Botham, the great all-rounder, was given the opportunity but failed. He was an altogether different cup of tea from Trevor, though. With Bailey, a sense of responsibility was etched deep into the character. Nobody could quite say that of Botham.

Come the end of 1953, with an enviable (if initially gradual) curve of success since his first Test match in 1949 behind him, Bailey had become almost the first name to be written down when the selectors came to pick their side. Home or away, whatever the opposition – the world was his oyster, at least until 1954, when along came the piece of grit which produced not the legendary pearl, but rather an irritation which, sharply painful at the time, still remains with him in subdued form. But there were no signs of this, no small speck on the horizon when, having brought the Ashes back to England for the first time in twenty years, Len Hutton and his team flew out to play in the West Indies in the early months of 1954, with Bailey as vice-captain. With Hutton fighting occasional bouts of ill-health, the prospects for Trevor Edward Bailey looked to be limitless.

The 1953–54 tour of West Indies was beset by problems on and off the field. Len Hutton vowed that what happened to him and to the team he captained shortened his own cricketing life by two years. Certainly, there have been tours since then beset by similar problems, but this one, because of the way in which problems surfaced, in the very nature of the incidents themselves and in the total unpreparedness of the touring team to cope with those events, was unique in its ugliness.

Inter-island rivalry was at its height. This went hand in hand with a mounting surge towards power for the black peoples which the local whites were keen to allay. The Caribbean whites still controlled cricket, but their time was short-lived. Those who clung desperately to the last vestiges of colonial power made little secret of their wish that England would win. Members of the MCC team were constantly reminded of the fact. Some also – strange as it seems from the distance of the 1990s – resented that England had seen fit to tour with a professional captain,

and that West Indies should have been seen as a place suitable for such
an experiment.

The 1955 *Wisden* summed up the position as follows:

'To set out the origins and assess the responsibilities for the
tension which marred so much of MCC's tour of the West
Indies in the early months of 1954 is anything but simple.
Certainly, the early insistence of so many people that the
'cricket championship of the world' was at stake did nothing to
ease the situation. Nor did the constant emphasis on victory
which the MCC players found to be stressed by English
residents there. A certain amount of tension was thus created
before a ball had been bowled. This quickly became heightened
through crowds, whose intense noise, coupled with almost
ceaseless torrid heat, provided a background in which tempers
too easily became frayed. At times some crowds were
demonstrative, and twice they became menacing. Convinced by
the happenings on the field that the general standard of
umpiring in the West Indies was not adequate for Test cricket,
the touring team felt that the crowd atmosphere made the work
of the men in the middle even harder than it should have been.
The MCC players sympathised with the umpires threatened
with physical violence, as marred the first and third Tests.
When, as the West Indies players admitted, the majority of
disputed decisions, usually at moments of match crisis, went
against MCC, they wondered how in the circumstances any
umpire could remain completely calm and controlled.

'To a man, the MCC team recognised their responsibilities as
ambassadors of sport but, being human, the less phlegmatic did
not always hide their annoyance and displeasure. In some
instances only someone with the forbearance of the most highly
trained diplomat could have been expected to preserve absolute
sangfroid. Dramatic gestures of disappointment and untactful
remarks, however understandable some of them were in the

heat of the moment, caused resentment among West Indies officials, umpires and others. No doubt some of the 'incidents' were exaggerated, but to deny their existence . . . would be only a disservice to the future welfare of the game.'

Nor was the England party chosen as wisely as it might have been. Len Hutton himself was certain that the team had been selected too hurriedly, were unaware of what awaited them and had been inadequately briefed. Nor was the management on the spot, in the shape of Charles Palmer, up to the task of placating the troops and calming the natives. To be fair, it is difficult to know who would have been, such was the diversity of problems encountered. But it did not help that Palmer had never been to the Caribbean and knew few, if any, people there. He had been given the somewhat invidious position of player-manager. Never a happy combination of roles, it was a nigh impossible charge in the conditions that confronted the MCC cricketers in 1953–54. The manager needs to be able to stand back from the day-to-day fray and exert his authority from a distance, however small. Palmer was pleasant, conciliatory, but out of his depth in an atmosphere reeking of tension, in Jamaica and British Guiana especially. Hutton needed a powerful, detached figure to take the burden of off-the-field incidents from his shoulders, and he did not have one.

As it was, Palmer's activities on the field were strictly limited. He played in one Test match, chosen ahead of Sussex's Ken Suttle – to the annoyance, not hidden, of such as Fred Trueman, who saw nepotism in the choice – and in only two more matches. Among other matters, it was the truculence of Trueman, who struck up anything but a happy understanding with his Yorkshire team-mate and captain on the tour, and the development of several other contentious issues as the series progressed, which kept Palmer more than busy, if not wholly effective.

The on-field history of the tour, with its undertones of a 'bouncer war' and a fight for the 'world championship' going hand in hand with crowds becoming intoxicated in the sizzling sun, and umpires sometimes in fear opf retribution from those who lost bets as a result of a crucial decision, was similarly unhappy. There was a riot in British Guiana, umpiring flawed by incompetence as well as by fear, and there were misunderstandings on every side. In the face of all this, Hutton's side moved from match to match increasingly unhappily. They lost the first two Tests. Even the equable Tom Graveney demonstrably lost his temper on one occasion in Port-of-Spain. Younger players, such as Fred Trueman and Tony Lock, were subsequently accused of im-mature behaviour off the field. The touring party, not wishing to be overwhelmed by official functions, had put a limit on them at Hutton's request, and umbrage was taken, Hutton blamed.

Compared with much that has happened since on Test tours in various parts of the world, the incidents seem relatively commonplace. In the context of late 1953, they were virtually unheard of, shocking even. But the cricket went on. Hutton became increasingly unhappy with events both on the field and off it. In his attempts to marshal his resources to do what he, the first professional captain of England, had set out to do, he had the backing of an amateur vice-captain who gave him the fullest support, born of professional instincts second to none. This was not always geared to the most accommodating attitude towards West Indies on the field. Statesmen back at Lord's might have expected a less confrontational approach and they did not get it. Nor for a long time did it lead to success on the field. Both in terms of style and the results achieved, MCC were open to criticism, even if a fair amount of it was misdirected.

Trevor Bailey was, above all, dedicated to winning. *Playing to Win* was the title of the book which appeared in his name shortly after this tour, and it was more than an eye-catching phrase. It was a philosophy. Not that this meant playing to win at all costs; far from it. Always scrupulously fair within the laws and spirit of the game, Trevor was nevertheless dedicated to beating the opposition, and to using all his powers of thought and deed, both possessed in great measure, to that end. His was a professional approach, just as much as that of Len Hutton, but unencumbered by such inherent worries of placating the mandarins at Lord's as formed an essential part of Len's make-up. For all his reliance upon the game for a living, Trevor

79

Edward Bailey was his own man. He was also a great source of support for Hutton.

Drawing the line between winning and what Reg Hayter, writing on the tour in the *Wisden* of 1955, described with insight in the following manner will have cost Trevor little sleep. It plainly cost Len a great deal. 'In the arrangement of tours,' wrote Hayter, 'Marylebone Cricket Club always has set the furtherance of friendship between man and man, country and country, as one of its main hopes and objectives. MCC firmly maintain their idealistic outlook that the spirit in which the game is played carries greater importance than such transient elation or disappointment as the winning or losing of a Test series . . . Whatever the gains in other directions, the primary intention for the tour was not fulfilled, and the circumstances of its failure were such that all those with the welfare of cricket at heart realised that the problems arising needed to be tackled quickly and without heat.'

Problems arising indeed. In those tranquil days when the amateur approach was still recognised as having value, even in the professional ranks of English cricketers, a genuine dichotomy existed. The urge to win fairly and squarely was paramount. But the England cricketer in the Caribbean had to be above reproach if he was to escape criticism, unfair though that often may have been. All England's cricketers with much experience were aware of that, none more than Hutton and Bailey at their head. Yet whichever way they turned, some new, unforeseen incident reared its head. They did their best to deal diplomatically but, as individual members of the team occasionally snapped under the burden of what they deemed to be provocation, they were left in the end with going flat out to win and letting the other considerations take care of themselves. Bailey's own reflections include the following:

'Like so many England teams we were slightly arrogant and distinctly intolerant of the accommodation provided and some of the administrative arrangements. These were the responsibility of the West Indies Board of Control who, as they were paying for it, tried to cut the costs to a minimum. The

situation was not helped by the West Indian side itself being
rather divided by both colour and island differences. In those days
it was inconceivable to stage a Test at any of the four major
grounds – Sabina Park, Kensington Oval, Bourda and Queen's
Park Oval – without including at least two locals in the XI, so that
politics, not cricket, governed the selection of the West Indies
team. When we returned home I hardly knew Weekes, Worrell
and Walcott, with whom I was to become so friendly later.'

As if the organisational shortcomings at the grounds, the peculiar
political situation and the low standard of umpiring were not enough,
there was also the superb form of the three W's – Walcott, Worrell and
Weekes – to contend with, as well as the continuing menace of 'those
little pals of mine', Sonny Ramadhin and Alf Valentine. Then, among
others, there was J. K. Holt, a Jamaican batsman of rare gifts who came
into his own before the first Test match and rarely failed against the
tourists.

It was a cauldron in which the MCC team of 1953–54 were in danger
of being done to a frazzle. And for a long time, following a false dawn
which brought victory by an innings in their first match against
Jamaica, it looked as though they would be in for a roasting. England
lost the first Test by 140 runs. Bailey batted for three and a half hours in
the match without being dismissed, but more than that was needed on a
pitch which belied its looks, lacking the pace expected by England
when they picked four fast bowlers. Statham bowled magnificently, as
he was to do throughout the tour but, needing 457 to win in the final
innings and having reached 227 for 2, England were undone by the
negative tactics employed by Jeffrey Stollmeyer, the West Indies
captain. Seven men on the leg side and Esmond Kentish, the fast-
medium bowler, bowling on or outside the leg stump caused May on 69
to lose patience and the rest, except for Trevor, fell in a heap.

Losing the Test was one thing. Attacks on the family of the umpire
who gave out Holt, the local hero, lbw within 6 runs of a century in his
first Test was quite another. Unsettling, too, was the manifestation of
inter-island rivalry which broke out when Stollmeyer (from Trinidad)

failed to enforce the follow-on and was greeted by continual booing. West Indies had grown accustomed to those local difficulties; the England players found them disturbing. No more unsettling, though, than when Lock, the only spinner in the team, was no-balled for throwing during the second West Indies innings. This was not a case of bad umpiring; more a 'fair cop'. But it was also in the nature of a sudden shock, and Lock's faster ball, a formidable weapon in his armoury, was put under wraps for the rest of the tour under instructions from Hutton. That it should resurface during the English cricket season of 1954 and that Doug Insole, captain of Essex, should have had his stumps spreadeagled by it and, turning to the square-leg umpire, should enquire politely whether he had been given 'run out', is a different story. But it was widely thought at the time that Lockie chucked his quicker ball.

Anyhow, it was not a good start to the series. Along with others, Trevor was concerned for Hutton's peace of mind under all the pressure and tried to bolster his captain's self-confidence by doing all he could to raise his spirits by talking the game, talking victory. It was something they both understood. But the second Test was also lost, by 181 runs. Bridgetown, Barbados, should have been a happy enough hunting-ground for batsmen of the calibre of Hutton, Watson, May, Compton and Graveney. And Statham, Bailey, Lock and Laker were the nucleus of a fine attack. Yet Statham's continued excellence, an encouraging bowling performance by Laker, two 70s by Hutton and good second innings by Compton, May and Graveney were not enough in the face of the first-innings shackles inspired by Ramadhin and Valentine. There was no recovery for England after they had been rendered almost strokeless in their first innings.

Faced by a total of 383, England's caution on a good pitch for batting was incomprehensible. Neither Hutton nor Bailey were averse to the theory that 'occupation of the crease wins matches', but the scoring of 128 runs from 114 overs on the third day of this match was doomed to produce the opposite result. Far from grinding down West Indies, these tactics gave them all the confidence in the world. Even a more freely conceived and executed approach in the second innings could not retrieve the situation, beyond restoring some sort of balance to an England side whose poise had been severely shattered. Trevor Bailey himself did not have the happiest of matches. He dislocated a finger during the first West Indies innings and played in some pain throughout the next four days.

Bailey was, however, a foremost mover in organising a dinner party soon after this defeat in the second Test had left England two down with three to play. It had become all too apparent that some of the older players thought Hutton's approach too defensive, and that he in turn thought that they were not giving 100 per cent. This was certainly not a stricture that Len would have applied to Bailey, but it was plain that something had to be done about this, and about bringing the party closer together. There was a lack of understanding and rapport between the old guard and the new, and it needed to be resolved.

It was a dinner of significance. Bailey and Compton were among those who made it clear to the captain that he had their support come what may, persuaded him that a more aggressive attitude on the field could profitably be adopted, and made it clear that they would do everything in their power to align the whole team, young and old, solidly behind him. Hutton was greatly heartened.

It was, even more, adversity that turned the tide for England. In the long run, it was as much stubborn pride as their undoubted ability which brought them through. Trevor describes matters and events at about this time:

'Two-nil down with three matches to go against the strongest batting line-up in the world was not the most encouraging position. In these circumstances it was hardly surprising that we had been written off by the popular press because our performances on the field had not been good enough, and also by Jim Swanton and most of the so-called serious press because we had also failed to lose with the apologetic grace and false smile of a civil servant from a minor public school. The outlook was bleak and, to make it bleaker, the next stop was British

Guiana which, unlike most of the West Indies, has little to
recommend it apart from the airport when you are about to
depart. However, it was here that our comeback began.

'Although we thrashed the Guiana team by an innings and 98
runs, we were unhappy about the standard of the umpiring, which
was worse than that experienced in Jamaica and Barbados. We
therefore requested another pair for the [third] Test, and
suggested Burke from Jamaica and Walcott from Barbados.
Considering we had lost when they had officiated we could hardly
have been fairer, but the local Board felt it to be a reflection on
their own umpires, which it was not – merely a condemnation. In
the end we settled for the local groundsman, Menzies, and
Gillette, who had said he would never umpire a Test again after
the Indians had been rude to him the previous year. This oddly
chosen pair proved to be efficient, while we started our recovery as
a result of producing our best all-round performance.'

The team was steeled in that third Test by the actions of the crowd in
British Guiana when they threw bottles, invaded the pitch and
generally showed misplaced displeasure at the umpire's decision when
giving the local man, Clifford McWatt, run out on the fourth day.
Bailey and others implored Hutton not to accede to a request by the
British Guiana President that the team should leave the field. Hutton
had no intention of doing so, and his remark that he wanted to get a
couple of West Indians out before close of play was beautifully apt in
the circumstances. For, by then, England were in an incontestible
position barring acts of God or the crowd. Hutton had made 169 of his
team's first-innings 435; Bailey had the third highest score with 49.
West Indies were on the run after Statham took 3 early wickets in the
first innings and, with the great Frank Worrell failing twice in the
match, England won comfortably by 9 wickets.

For the fourth Test, played at Port-of-Spain, Trinidad, Bailey was
picked as an opening batsman. The reasons at the time were not all that
obvious. Willie Watson had gone in with Hutton previously in the
Tests with a fair degree of success. Bailey had been there in the normal

all-rounder's spot in the middle of the order shoring up the innings, a job accomplished with great success in the previous Test. The answer lay only partly in Bailey's successful venture in the role of opener in the island match against Trinidad that preceded the Test. Peter May had opened in the first innings without success, but Watson had made 141 going in at No. 3. Why, then, did Bailey open the innings in the Test and not Watson?

Trevor always felt that Hutton saw him as the one he would most like to open with – a matter of style and what Hutton saw as the right technique: the initial forward movement which Hutton himself employed. There was also, of course, Hutton's inbuilt feeling, matured over the years, that Trevor was second to none in his possession of, in his words, 'the nerve and tactical skill to stand up to the new ball and, with luck, give England a start or two.' What Len wanted in the Caribbean heat was occupation of the crease. In Trevor he saw his best chance of achieving that. On the reverse of the coin, Len also felt that, with his limited range of strokes, Bailey was not seen to best advantage in the second half of the order.

Both sides of Trevor's character were seen in the pre-Test Trinidad match. MCC needed 231 to win in four and a quarter hours on a slow wicket. Only 78 runs came in the first two hours. Then Bailey sprang a surprise, as he was sometimes wont to do. He raced to 90, hitting one huge six they still talk about out there, and setting up the innings for Compton and Watson to put on 60 in half an hour. MCC won with twenty-five minutes to spare, and Trevor's place as an opening batsman was booked for the last two Test matches.

The Port-of-Spain Test match, played on the mat, was a holiday for batsmen. For the first time in the series, the three Ws all fired together, making between them 497 of the 681 scored by West Indies, who declared just before lunch on the third day. Bailey played his part in achieving the formidable task of saving the follow-on, making 46 before Compton and May both made centuries and Graveney 92. England ended the game one down with one to go – and a rib injury had left them without their most successful bowler, Brian Statham, since the first morning. The scorecard on page 92 tells the story.

This match was virtually back to back with the final Test at Kingston, Jamaica, so that Statham was unfit for that too. So it was that Bailey, having filled in the one remaining match – a two-day fixture against the Jamaica Colts – by scoring 55 on a nasty, flying, sticky wicket, out of MCC's total of 135, came to open the bowling and the batting in the fifth Test. England needed to win to level the series. By now there were many other reasons why they needed to win. They needed to prove that all the problems which had beset them throughout the tour had not diverted them sufficiently from their course to cause them to return home empty-handed. There was honour and pride at stake, and a great need to support Hutton at the end of what for him, especially, had been a tour trying almost beyond endurance. Bailey was to do that in no small measure.

Before the opportunity arose, however, the England players were treated with icy indifference by the Jamaican authorities. Len Hutton was upset by the way the promise of the usual complimentary tickets for the players was dishonoured. The knives were out for Len, he felt. He did not feel any better when he lost the toss on a perfect batting wicket. Hutton himself takes up the story:

'The most extraordinary feature of Bailey's inspired bowling in the first West Indies innings, which got us on the victory path, was that everything was wrong for him. On the day before the Test I had looked at the pitch with the groundsman, who said that the side batting first ought to make 700. Looking at the strip, rolled and rolled again until it shone under the Caribbean sun, I was inclined to agree; I thought England's only chance was to win the toss, aim for 400-plus, and hope by some miracle to bowl West Indies out twice. My feelings can be imagined when I lost the toss . . . and the miracle occurred with the opposition routed for an unbelievable 139 by Bailey, who had 7 for 34 in the sixteen best overs he ever bowled. Bailey rates this as his best performance, and no one would venture to disagree. There was a little bit of moisture in the pitch left over from the watering, but the interesting fact is that

1. Trevor Bailey at seventeen, wearing his 'colours' blazer at Dulwich College. By then he was captain of the cricket XI, captain of squash and in the XV

2. Going out to bat for Essex v. Gloucestershire at Chalkwell Park, Westcliff in 1947. The young Bailey's worried frown signifies a crisis. Untypically, Bailey was stumped for 7, so this was one crisis he did not overcome

3. A batsman's eye view of Bailey in May, 1950 just prior to his delivery stride and at the end of the final leap. He has apparently moved wide of the crease in order to slant the ball towards the leg side

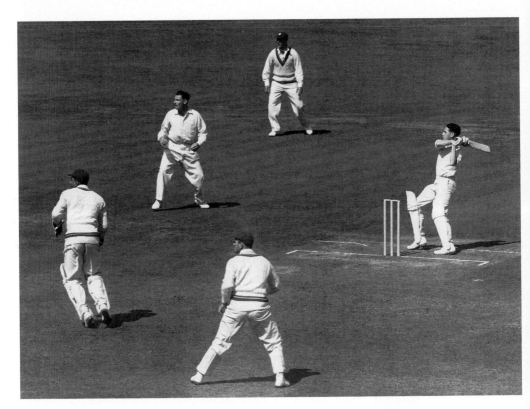

4. A bouncer from Prior Jones, the West Indies fast bowler, is helped on its way to the boundary by Bailey in the final Test match of the 1950 series at the Oval

5. Bailey hits Bill Johnston for 4 during his defiant 71 against Australia at Lord's on 30 June, 1953. It was an innings which, with Willie Watson's century, saved the match against all odds and kept England's quest for the Ashes alive

6. Trevor Bailey (right) and Willie Watson, pictured outside 'Q' stand at Lord's after their epic partnership in the 1953 Lord's Test against Australia. Over five hours at the crease has plainly made Willie more tired than Trevor

7. Bailey is at the right end for this delivery from Ray Lindwall, the great Australian fast bowler, during the final Test of the 1953 series at the Oval

8. Bailey making progress with a square cut for 4, bringing him his half century against Australia at the Oval in 1953. This innings played an important part in England's victory and the recapture of the Ashes

9. Essex in 1954. Back row: (left to right) H. Dalton (masseur), G. Barker, P. A. Gibb, P. Cousens, W. T. Greensmith, K. C. Preston, B. Taylor. Front row: J. A. Bailey, T. E. Bailey, D. J. Insole, R. Smith, T. C. Dodds, R. Horsfall

10. Most Australians are delighted with Neil Harvey's catch to dismiss Bailey in Archer's leg trap at Lord's in the second Test of the 1956 series. However, Keith Miller, hands on hips at first slip, appears matter-of-fact and unsurprised. Peter May is the non-striker

11. The end of a superb catch in which Bailey dived forward and to his right to take the ball inches off the ground in the first Test match v. South Africa in Johannesburg in December 1956. Clive van Ryneveld is the unfortunate batsman, Statham is the bowler. Evans and Cowdrey lead the applause

12. Bailey and Peter Richardson opened the batting in all five Tests in South Africa in 1956–57. Here, they are pictured going out to bat in England's first innings of the Durban Test. Bailey made 80, Richardson 68 of England's total of 218

13. The full face of the bat is shown to Surrey's Jim Laker on the last day of May, 1958 at the Oval. Arthur McIntyre and Ken Barrington look on with a sense of *déjà vu*

14. England v. New Zealand at Edgbaston in 1958. Back row: (*left to right*) P. E. Richardson, P. J. Loader, T. W. Graveney, M. J. K. Smith, G. A. R. Lock, M. C. Cowdrey, F. S. Trueman. Front row: T. G. Evans, P. B. H. May, T. E. Bailey, J. C. Laker

15. Derek Shackleton of Hampshire cannot get past that forward defensive stroke even with four stumps to aim at. Who better to conduct an experiment on behalf of MCC at Lord's in 1963 than these two, with Robin Hobbs at mid-on

16. Master and pupil. Bailey, captain of Essex, pictured in 1965 with his protégé, Barry Knight, who had by then established himself as an all-rounder in the England team but was soon to leave Essex for Leicestershire

17. Five generations of Essex captains celebrate the opening of the new indoor cricket school at Chelmsford in 1992. From left: Graham Gooch, Doug Insole, Brian Taylor, Tom Pearce, Trevor Bailey and Keith Fletcher

the cross-breeze actually did not favour him, nor presumably had Statham been fit and played – an injury problem which entailed the inclusion of three spinners – would he have opened with Trueman.

'As Trueman was the faster bowler, Bailey had to bowl against the wind (it is also a thought that, if Bedser had been there, Bailey would have started at the other end!) and the cross-wind was also in the wrong direction for Bailey's out-swingers . . . Trueman, of course, also bowled the out-swinger so, in theory, he had all the advantages. "When I started I would gladly have settled for, say, 3 for 100," says Trevor. One gropes for an alternative phrase to the old cliché about cricket's glorious uncertainties, but surely the time-honoured words fit the case and, once again, Bailey was shown to be one of the most capable and intelligent cricketers of our times. He was every captain's ideal: responsive, perceptive, guaranteed to be a tactical move ahead of his shrewdest opponent, and never overawed or intimidated. Unlike too many English players, he was able to play to the maximum of his ability on the big occasions. Ask him to attack with the new ball, and he would stretch the skill of any batsman because of his complete mastery of the basics; ask him to bowl tight, and he would do precisely that; ask him to open the batting to blunt the attack for the stroke-makers, and he would be there fighting every inch of the way; ask him to field close or away from the bat, and he'd be equally proficient. A fine all-rounder, and his service to England cannot be overestimated.'

Trevor Bailey's 7 for 34 was a blow from which West Indies never recovered, and the knife was rammed home and twisted by a superb double century from Hutton when England took strike for the first time. Hutton batted for little short of nine hours in compiling 205, the only double century made hitherto by an England captain on a tour abroad. Hutton and Bailey between them had been largely responsible for England's nine-wicket victory.

Hutton's delight in squaring the series was marred by what for him

West Indies v England. Fifth Test at Kingston, Jamaica. March 30, 31 April 1, 2, 3, 1954

West Indies

J. K. Holt c Lock b Bailey	0	— c Lock b Trueman	8
J. B. Stollmeyer c Evans b Bailey	9	— lbw b Trueman	64
E. Weekes b Bailey	0	— b Wardle	3
F. M. Worrell c Wardle b Trueman	4	— c Graveney b Trueman	29
C. L. Walcott c Laker b Lock	50	— c Graveney b Laker	116
D. Atkinson lbw b Bailey	21	— c Watson b Bailey	40
G. E. Gomez c Watson b Bailey	4	— lbw b Laker	22
C. McWatt c Lock b Bailey	22	— c Wardle b Laker	8
G. Sobers not out	14	— c Compton b Lock	26
F. King b Bailey	9	— not out	10
S. Ramadhin lbw b Trueman	4	— c and b Laker	10
L-b 1, n-b 1	2	B 4, 1-b 3, w 1, n-b 2	10

1/0 2/2 3/13 4/13 5/65 6/75   139   1/26 2/38 3/102 4/123   346
7/110 8/115 9/133   5/191 6/273 7/293 8/306 9/326

England

L. Hutton c McWatt b Walcott	205		
T. E. Bailey c McWatt b Sobers	23		
P. B. H. May c sub b Ramadhin	30	— not out	40
D. C. S. Compton hit wkt b King	31		
W. Watson c McWatt b King	4	— not out	20
T. W. Graveney lbw b Atkinson	11		
T. G. Evans c Worrell b Ramadhin	28		
J. H. Wardle c Holt b Sobers	66		
G. A. R. Lock b Sobers	4		
J. C. Laker b Sobers	9	— b King	0
F. S. Trueman not out	0		
L-b 3	3	B 12	12

1/43 2/104 3/152 4/160 5/179 6/287   414   1/0   (1 wkt.)   72
7/392 8/401 9/406

England Bowling

	O.	M.	R.	W.	O.	M.	R.	W
Bailey	16	7	34	7	25	11	54	1
Trueman	15.4	4	39	2	29	7	88	3
Wardle	10	1	20	0	39	14	83	1
Lock	15	6	31	1	27	15	40	1
Laker	4	1	13	0	50	27	71	4

West Indies Bowling

	O.	M.	R.	W.	O.	M.	R.	W
King	26	12	45	2	4	1	21	1
Gomez	25	8	56	0				
Atkinson	41	15	82	1	3	0	8	0
Ramadhin	29	9	71	2	3	0	14	0
Sobers	28.5	9	75	4	1	0	6	0
Walcott	11	5	26	1				
Worrell	11	0	34	0	4	0	8	0
Stollmeyer	5	0	22	0				
Weekes					0.5	0	3	0

Umpires: P. Burke and T. Ewart.

was the final straw – a groundless accusation that he had insulted the Chief Minister of Jamaica by failing to acknowledge the congratulations of Alex Bustamente as he made his way from the field to the dressing-room. Bustamente himself made it clear that he had not been nor had he felt insulted. But this did not prevent the matter being blown up into a local storm, nor did it prevent an official from bursting into the England dressing-room and talking of the incident as the 'crowning insult'. This was more then enough for Hutton's sensitive character, and it was with a sense of relief that he embarked for England, leaving petty local politics behind him.

For Bailey the tour had been something of a watershed. His enormous all-round ability had been confirmed; his singular talents were widely recognised; Hutton had seen him as the best man of those on tour to open the batting with him (his stay of two and a half hours in England's first innings of the final Test wore down West Indies' only really fast bowler, Frank King, who bowled many more balls to him than to Hutton); and it was by no means a wild stretch of the imagination on the part of those who saw him as the heir-apparent to the England captaincy when and if Hutton relinquished the post through ill-health or – if the West Indies tour were any guide – sheer disillusionment. For Bailey had achieved a batting average of nearly 39 runs in the Test matches. He had finished second only to Statham as a bowler. He was widely acknowledged as a shrewd tactician and a fine close fielder. To the public he was a hero, to his fellow players a man who would never let them down. But the 'golden boy' image was to receive a severe dent, not long after the return to England and the onset of a new season, with Pakistan the visitors, in 1954.

Throughout his cricketing career, Trevor supplemented his earnings by writing articles on the game. He had, for some time, contributed modest but informative pieces to *The Cricketer* and other publications. As a new recruit to the Essex team at the tail-end of 1953, during his wonderful series against Australia, I had been surprised to see the great man leaving dinner to type up another piece, had come across him in the hotel lounge thumping away at his battered machine. It seemed a hard, busy life.

89

Quite apart from his various articles, he was also engaged in writing his book *Playing to Win*. It was published in 1954, and it seems certain that it cost Bailey the England captaincy – or at least its serialisation in the *People* newspaper did; for the one bore only passing relationship to the other.

As Trevor tells it – and he is most reluctant to do so – the *People*, anxious to cash in on the popular hero of the hour, approached him with a view to serialisation, prevailing upon him to add a chapter on the recently completed tour of the West Indies. For the first, and only, time in his life, he acceded to their request that a ghost writer should be employed. Time pressed, and there could be no harm, Trevor thought, in what he had to say being translated into popular tabloidese by the ghost writer in question, since it was his brother, Basil, a journalist with the evening *Star*, who was to be responsible.

When that particular edition of the *People* surfaced it horrified not only those flitting up and down the corridors of power at Lord's, but also those with the best interests of T. E. Bailey at heart. For the article bore little resemblance to what Basil Bailey had written. Although Trevor had reserved the right to vet the article, it was not until the Saturday before publication on the Sunday that he became even half-aware of the dangerous slant that could be put on some of the incidents described in his book or of the ingenious way matters could be taken out of context and given undue emphasis. By then it was too late, and he was too far away for anything to be done about it; and the highlighting of some of the more controversial issues arising out of the recent tour of the West Indies – and there had been plenty of them – appeared on the breakfast tables of millions, in distorted form.

The book itself was innocuous enough, although it did refer to matches which had taken place not only in West Indies, but during the Australian tour of England in 1953. Both series fell within the restricted period of two years which those under contract for inter-national cricket undertook not to comment on publicly. The fact was, though, that in Bailey's case, since he played as an amateur, no contract worth the name existed. He remains adamant that no provisions of any such agreement were broken, although he does bitterly regret allowing the material to fall into the wrong hands.

It was apparent, sitting as I was in the same dressing-room soon after the England team to play Pakistan in the second Test beginning on 1st July 1954 had been announced, that the appointment of David Sheppard as captain was a blow to Trevor, and one which would take him some time to absorb. Len Hutton's ill-health and subsequent loss of form had caused him to inform the selectors of his unavailability for the Test during the match between Middlesex and Yorkshire, when the team had already been selected. Bailey had been Hutton's vice-captain in the West Indies, had captained MCC against Pakistan with considerable flair and, although selected for the second Test, now saw Sheppard drafted in as captain over his head – although he, Sheppard, had not played in the first Test.

It was as big a slap in the teeth as could be imagined for somebody at the peak of his career. Bailey must have known that the final accolade, the captaincy of his country, was now unlikely ever to come his way. After that week at Romford, Essex moved on to Gloucester, but Trevor was not with us. He and Greta spent a long week-end in Paris, where the French neither knew nor cared.

It may well be wondered why one slip such as this should have cost him the most coveted job in English cricket for ever. The truth may well lie not so much in those articles published in the Sunday tabloid as in his pertinent, though often critical, observations which drew attention to organisational deficiencies in tour arrangements generally and MCC's part in them particularly. The treatment of the professional cricketers taking part in tours, and the financial arrangements and the disadvantages he felt English cricket was placed under by them, were just two items calculated to anger such administrators as Gubby Allen. And after that, unless you were prepared to eat a largish portion of humble pie, the way back could be long and hard.

Trevor was not disposed to such a diet, and a cool distance between him and the powerful Gubby was rarely bridged. Trevor, in his maturity, affects to be quite content with having captained England only once – in an England v Australia computerised Test match. But there is a wry smile when he tells you so.

West Indies v England. Fourth Test at Port-of-Spain, Trinidad. March 17, 18, 19, 20, 22, 23, 1955

West Indies

J. K. Holt c Compton b Trueman	40			
J. B. Stollmeyer c and b Compton	41			
E. D. Weekes c Bailey b Lock	206	— c sub b Trueman	1
F. M. Worrell b Lock	167	— c sub b Lock	56
C. L. Walcott c and b Laker	124	— not out	51
B. Pairaudeau run out	0	— hit wkt b Bailey	5
D. Atkinson c Graveney b Compton	74	— not out	53
C. McWatt b Laker	4		
W. Ferguson not out	8	— b Bailey	44
B 6, l-b 4, n-b 3	17	L-b 2	2

1/78 2/92 3/430 4/517   (8 wkts., dec.)   681   1/19 2/20   (4 wkts., dec.)   212

5/540 6/627 7/641 8/681   3/72 4/111

S. Ramadhin and F. King did not bat.

England

L. Hutton c Ferguson b King	44	— not out	30
T. E. Bailey c Weekes b Ferguson	46		
P. B. H. May c Pairaudeau b King	135	— c Worrell b McWatt	16
D. C. S. Compton c and b Ramadhin	133		
W. Watson c Atkinson b Walcott	4	— c Ferguson b Worrell	32
T. W. Graveney c and b Walcott	92	— not out	0
R. T. Spooner b Walcott	19	— c Ferguson b Ramadhin	16
J. C. Laker retired hurt	7		
G. A. R. Lock lbw b Worrell	10		
F. S. Trueman lbw b King	19		
J. B. Statham not out	6		
B 10, 1-b 5, w 7	22	L-b 4	4

1/73 2/135 3/301 4/314 5/424 6/493   537   1/52 2/52 3/83   (3 wkts.)   98

7/496 8/510 9/537

England Bowling

	O.	M.	R.	W.		O.	M.	R.	W.
Statham	9	0	31	0					
Trueman	33	3	131	1	....	15	5	23	1
Bailey	32	7	104	0	....	12	2	20	2
Laker	47	8	154	2					
Lock	59	14	178	2	....	10	2	40	1
Compton	9.4	1	40	2	....	7	0	51	0
Graveney	3	0	26	0	....	5	0	33	0
Hutton						6	0	43	0

West Indies Bowling

	O.	M.	R.	W.		O.	M.	R.	W.
King	48	16	97	3					
Worrell	20	2	58	1	....	9	1	29	1
Ramadhin	34	13	74	1	....	7	4	6	1
Atkinson	32	12	60	0	....	4	0	12	0
Ferguson	47	17	155	1					
Stollmeyer	6	2	19	0					
Walcott	34	18	52	3					
Weekes						5	1	28	0
McWatt						4	1	16	1
Pairaudeau						1	0	3	0

Umpires: K. Woods and E. Achong.

5

England and Essex
and a Winter in Australia

1954–55

For Bailey, not knowing what a furore his book was to cause, the landscape was fresh and clean when the 1954 season began. The emergent country of Pakistan were playing their first Test series in England and, in those days, though full of natural pride, were not considered the most formidable opposition. All eyes belonging to those in the international reckoning were on the coming tour to Australia and New Zealand during the winter of 1954–55. The summer of 1954 seemed a season to consolidate, to keep oneself firmly in the running and Bailey started by doing just that.

His selection to captain MCC against the tourists was no surprise, and he began the season on entirely the right foot. He led MCC with enterprise, declaring twice in an attempt to force a result on a good batting pitch and, having set Pakistan to get 80 an hour to win in two and a half hours, contrived to reduce them to 85 for 6 wickets by the close. His captaincy was both shrewd and imaginative, and his second-innings analysis, achieved when Pakistan were going for runs, is worth recording. It was eleven overs, seven maidens, 5 runs, 1 wicket.

The first Test match, in May and, most unusually, at Lord's, brought little benefit to anyone. Play was restricted to eight hours and, for nearly six of these, the Lord's crowd was treated to the sight of Hanif Mohammad making a total of 59 very slow runs in his two innings. Bailey bowled nine overs in the match and took 1 wicket for 14 runs, but perished in a frantic chase for runs before Hutton declared

England's first innings closed, and the weather intervened again to render a low-scoring game meaningless.

By the time the second Test at Nottingham had come round, the *People* had been published, the book was on sale, the selectors had acted, and Trevor was playing under David Sheppard. Sheppard's accession to Hutton's temporarily vacated throne sent Trevor psychologically if briefly into eclipse. Indeed, there were many at the time who were hoping that Sheppard, the 'real' amateur, might prove more than a temporary occupant of the captain's berth. Hutton's position, dogged as he was by illness and the various problems which had beset the recent tour of the West Indies, was far from secure. Bailey's book, well though it was selling, had blotted his copy and, for many, Sheppard had become the great white hope.

Victory for England by an innings in the second Test was no great surprise, but it did add fuel to the flames kindled by the amateur-at-any-cost lobby. England were by far the stronger side, and it was in this match that Denis Compton chose to play an innings of remarkable dimensions, even for him. It says much for Bailey's ability to focus unremittingly on the job in hand, when it came to Test-match cricket, that he should have been in complete command of the situation, perfectly attuned to the requirements of both his team and of Denis Compton. He came to the wicket with England on 339 for 4, Compton and Graveney having just added 154 in eighty-five minutes, and with Compton under full sail. Against a now thoroughly demoralised Pakistan attack, Bailey contrived, by deft placements and quick running, to give Compton nearly all the strike. By his self-denial, Bailey allowed Compton to score all but 27 of the 192 runs accruing from a partnership that lasted only an hour and three-quarters. The runs came faster during this partnership than at any other time, even faster than when Graveney was going full-tilt alongside Compton, and it had scarcely seemed possible that runs could come at a greater pace than that.

All this was, of course, a measure of Compton's mastery, but it was also a tribute to Trevor's tactical awareness – an awareness that Denis Compton (back to the form of those halcyon days before his knee had begun to trouble him) was like a fast-flowing river and that he, Bailey, should do everything in his power to encourage it to turn into a torrent. Into both their minds, in the latter stages of this stand, had come the possibility – faint, but nevertheless there – that Compton, who was riding majestically whatever luck came his way, could go on to beat Hutton's record Test innings of 364 runs, scored against Australia in 1938. In the end, Compton had to settle for 278, scored in four hours and fifty minutes, and the highest individual score made in a Test match at Nottingham. Trevor's undefeated 36 was dwarfed, scarcely mentioned, but it gave him considerable personal satisfaction; more, certainly, than his only three overs of a match which saw the emergence of Yorkshire's Bob Appleyard as a bowler of Test calibre, and the growing stature of Brian Statham as a bowler to be feared.

The third Test that year saw Bailey again pressed into service as an opening batsman, alongside Sheppard, with Hutton and Reg Simpson *hors de combat*. His versatility was seen to advantage in the 42 he made out of England's 359 for 8 in their only innings, before he became a victim of Denis Compton's eccentric running between the wickets. It was a match in which he was not called on to bowl. In fact, after being omitted from the fourth and final Test, though already chosen for the tour of Australia, he finished his three matches at international level against Pakistan having bowled only twelve overs. Two of these games had been under the captaincy of David Sheppard.

But, by then, the issue of the England captaincy had been resolved. Sheppard himself had been concerned by all the cloak-and-dagger manoeuvrings on staircases at Lord's and other pavilions up and down the country. Trevor had obviously been written off completely, and Errol Holmes of Surrey and Walter Robins, the former Middlesex captain, now a selector, were said to be in hot pursuit of securing a berth for Sheppard as captain of the team to Australia. Much intrigue notwithstanding, Len Hutton was finally reappointed and took with him as his vice-captain Peter May, who was to become one of England's greatest post-war batsmen. Such was Hutton's diffidence, however, so heavily had the cares of office weighed upon him, both at home against Australia in 1953 and in West Indies on the recent tour out there, that Sheppard had become convinced that Len would have been relieved if he, Sheppard, had been given the job. That's as may be. In the end, with some irony, David Sheppard was not even selected for the Australian tour as a batsman.

As vice-captain of Essex, Trevor more than pulled his weight. Although not a good year for his county, it was a magnificent one for him. He did the double, scoring 1,344 runs and taking 101 wickets in all matches, in a wet season, and with more than enough off-the-field worries to concern even him.

I had started playing for Essex at the tail-end of 1953 and was able to take off most of the summer of 1954 to play for the county. I had met Trevor and had played a couple of games with him in 1953. To my inexperienced and awe-filled eye, he had seemed in a world slightly apart from the rest of us. In those days in Essex, he was 'the man', the only current Test player, who would sail into the team between Test matches, score runs and take wickets, and then disappear again for a short spell. Then again, he was so busy when he wasn't actually playing. His battered typewritter could be heard click-clacking away in whatever hotel we were staying in for away matches. Not for him too many beers with the boys in the hotel bar, or too much reminiscing about the old days or players of yesteryear – and there was plenty of that in the Essex team. His priorities were different.

I met him first, as I say, at the tail-end of 1953. It was to his absence – he was at the Oval for the final Test against Australia – that I owed my first match as a young amateur against Nottinghamshire at Southend. I came into the team and stayed there throughout 1954 as the 'other Bailey', generally travelling with him and Doug Insole, the captain, in Doug's car from venue to venue. The trips were often long and seemed longer: Insole had the unnerving knack of peeling oranges with one hand while driving at 70 mph. I learned then from Trevor's demeanour in the front seat that not only was he absolutely fearless on the cricket field, but he was also something of a fatalist; for nothing, not even Doug Insole's driving, could disturb his equanimity. He knew where he was going and knew, absolutely, that he would get there. That attitude typified his cricket. His belief in himself and in his fate was perhaps his greatest asset.

So, throughout that 1954 season, I listened to any advice he would throw my way, which was infrequent but well worth the having; learned, when bowling, to use the crease and a number of variations; learned not to resent his always having the best of conditions when playing for Essex. He was the best bowler we had and he knew the idiosyncrasies of everyone we played against, and he passed on his knowledge if you asked him. He had by then settled for being a third seam bowler and utility batsman for England. For Essex he was much more.

Bailey and Insole were a pair. Their tastes off the field were the same. In the evenings, they would often disappear for a view of the local cinema's latest offering, especially if it was a western. I was of an age when I would be more enthralled by the stories the professionals told over a pint of bitter when play came to a close. But it was a happy team, Essex in 1954, even if the results, in a wet summer, with a leg-spinner as our only regular purveyor of spin attack, were patchy to poor. Every match, for someone living in the centre of London as I was, was an away match. I learned what it was like living in hotels in Essex and elsewhere, and I rather enjoyed it; enjoyed, too, the VIP treatment accorded to Essex players wherever in the county we pitched our tent for the week, such as free tickets to cinemas, or passes to Butlin's holiday camp in Clacton in the days when you were young and fancy-free.

I learned, too, why Trevor had become known, universally almost, as 'The Boil'. It had nothing to do with his personality, or the pain he inflicted on opponents. It had everything to do with a mispronunciation of his name by the announcer at a Swiss football match when the Cambridge soccer team were on tour. Bailey became 'Boiley' became 'the Boil' – a moniker which he has always appeared to accept with composure and a faint touch of pride. And I learned during that 1954 season to get used to the idea that Trevor would spend a fair bit of time on the massage table, with Harold 'Woozer' Dalton tending him with reverence and the utmost assiduousness for what seemed like a private patient's charter in a National Health dressing-room. I became used, too, to Doug Insole's frequent cry, in any sort of tactical dilemma, of

97

'What do you think, Boil?' Invariably, there would be a solemn pause, a lowering of the eyelds, and a wrinkling of the nose before Trevor would reply with advice, just as invariably taken.

The only time I can remember such advice being accompanied by raised eyebrows among the rest of the Essex team was one day at Edgbaston. It resulted in a change in the batting order which saw Frank Vigar, who was not then assured of a regular place in the side, going in as a sort of 'tea-watchman' in place of Trevor himself. Trevor would admit that he got it wrong that day.

Otherwise I learned to live with and grew to enjoy the Insole/ Bailey sense of humour, even though it left me somewhat embarrassed by happenings at Walthamstow Avenue Football Club one summer's evening. The three of us were travelling by car after a match at Leyton, destination Clacton. An arrival near midnight, even at Doug Insole's rate of driving, was a certainty, for *en route* Insole had promised to do the honours at the opening of the football club's new pavilion. We were greeted kindly by the club's chairman, who welcomed Doug and Trevor (until recently, a player of distinction for the club) while clearly not having the faintest idea who I was. Insole soon put that to rights: 'You know Trevor, of course,' he said, 'but I don't think you've met his son, Jack.' We shook hands all round, me towering above all three of them. Then came the time for speeches.

The chairman, among a number of other matters, was quick to allude to the debt owed to Doug Insole for finding the time to take part; welcomed Trevor, to applause; and then said that it was also good to see his son, Jack. There was a pause while everyone tried to identify Trevor's offspring. Surely not that tall, gangling bloke standing next to Trevor? Oblivious and regardless of the disbelief of his audience, the chairman moved on; and so did we, to Clacton. And, such were the vagaries of the fixture-list that year, from Clacton to Scarborough for the next match, and thence to Weston-super-Mare.

Trevor's achievement in doing the double in a wet season was a considerable one. By that stage in his career, it was unremarkable – it was something people had grown to expect – but it was quite a feat to take 100 wickets with his having bowled so few overs in the Tests which, for him, took six matches out of the season. He had earned his place on the boat to Australia.

In 1954, the MCC party still travelled to Australia by boat. It was a mode of transport which had its pros and cons for cricketers who needed to keep fit. There was every means of enjoyment on board, including vast quantities of food and drink. There was ample scope for exercise, too, but was there enough of the right kind? One thing does seem certain: as a means of getting to know your fellow-tourists it was without equal, and the team spirit could be bonded together in such a way as to serve the team well in the months ahead. For Trevor, the signs were auspicious.

In the first place, Len Hutton was in charge: Len whose faith in T. E. Bailey was unshakeable, Len who thought in similar fashion to Trevor about most cricketing matters and upon whom Trevor looked with great respect, not only because Len was possibly the greatest batsman in the world. Then there was his great friend, Reg Simpson; old, reliable buddies and wonderful cricketers in the shape of Evans, Compton, Edrich, Alec Bedser and Graveney; promising younger members in May, Colin Cowdrey, Frank Tyson and Statham. However, the omission of Willie Watson for Vic Wilson, his fellow Yorkshireman, yeoman fellow though Vic was, filled Trevor with astonishment at the time, as did the presence of Jim McConnon, the Glamorgan off-spinner, instead of the taciturn but immensely gifted Jim Laker.

As the only all-rounder in the party, Bailey was assured of a lot of cricket and a place in the Test team unless form deserted him. Hutton's faith in fast bowling, against the Australians or anyone else, was likely to be satisfied by the presence of the still-raw Tyson and the ever improving Statham. Tyson had created quite an impression in his first full season for Northamptonshire. After facing the new ball against him on a wet, slowish wicket at Rushden in June, Sonny Avery, the Essex opener, had given his own quiet verdict. He had spent about an hour at the crease. 'The fellow's quick,' he said, taking off his right-hand batting glove. 'It's a long time since I had one of these.' He pointed to the area between his thumb and forefinger, swollen and darkened by bruising: the result of the impact of ball upon bat and the constant jarring effect of getting behind the Typhoon's deliveries.

Trevor himself had occasion to find out how fast Tyson was. He had missed that match at Rushden. When Essex played Northamptonshire for a second time at Romford, he had made 34 when an express delivery sent his off stump flying. His defence mechanism was working in that game, however: he made 81 runs in the match for once out. But he had been given cause to hold Tyson in healthy respect.

The 1954–55 tour of Australia saw the consolidation of Bailey in his role as an essentially defensive cricketer at Test level. By now he was firmly established as a batsman whom the devil himself would have a job in shifting when it came to Test matches – especially against Australia – no matter where the game was played, no matter where he appeared in the order. The more he was criticised for slow scoring, the more he revelled in it. And, once Tyson had found himself, and he and Statham had become *enfants terribles*, Bailey's own natural niche was as an accurate fast-medium bowler, to pick up a few wickets or keep things quiet along with Bob Appleyard, while Tyson and Statham girded their loins for another onslaught. It did not always work out that way, but that was the general idea; it was a part Bailey could play to the hilt. He was as integral a part of Hutton's team as could be imagined in a game as uncertain as cricket.

Indeed, it was a feature of Bailey's first-class cricket career that he was always prepared, no, happy, to fill the breach, to do whatever was asked of him, especially if his acquiescence meant that he had a bigger part to play. The more dangerous or demanding it was, the better he liked it. Insole was unstinting in his praise for this aspect of Bailey's character. 'Trevor,' he said, 'possessed one very great asset from a captain's point of view. In an age of specialists, when so many good players insist on batting in their own favourite positions in the order, he has been conspicuous for his willingness to bat anywhere. In the England side he has plugged all the holes from 1 to 9, and has spent many hours with his pads on as nightwatchman or as a prospective steadying influence in the event of our losing an early wicket. For Essex, he moves up or down the order according to current needs or the state of a particular match.'

England's chances of retaining the Ashes they had captured in 1953 seemed, to the press, about even. Australia were without Hassett, their captain in England, and were led in his stead by the off-spinner, Ian Johnson. But they still possessed immense all-round strength: Miller, Davidson, Archer, Benaud, to name but a quartet. Apart from Bailey, Bedser and Statham, England's bowling was an unknown quantity when it came to Australian conditions, and Len Hutton had no difficulty in playing down the merits of his team when it came to an early press conference, after arriving in Australia.

The young Colin Cowdrey's impression of Len's masterly handling of the Australian press has been told often enough before, but bears repeating. It so captures Hutton's diffident and disarming way of dealing with potentially awkward issues:

'The Australian press, I suspect, were expecting a lot of bravado, even bombast. They received the opposite. When they phrased a question to bring a head-on collision, Hutton sat there, smiling slightly, turning the words over and over in his mind. Sometimes the pauses lasted fully thirty seconds and they became so long that twice at least Geoffrey Howard, the England team manager glanced round to see if the captain had fallen asleep. When the answer came it would be shrewd, pointed and drily witty. After about a dozen answers Hutton had them rolling in the gangways.

'It was all underplayed. "Noo, we 'aven't got mooch bowling. Got a chap called Tyson, but you won't 'ave 'eard of him because he's 'ardly ever played. Ah, yes, Lock and Laker. Aye, good boolers, but we 'ad to leave them behind (no explanation). Batsmen? Well, we 'aven't got any batsmen, really. We've got these youngsters, May and Cowdrey, but we haven't got any batsmen." Then wearily: "What it comes to is that we're startin' all over again. We've a lot to learn from you."

'They asked him what he thought of Australia's new-ball attack. Another long pause as he groped to try and remember

their names. "Oh, aye. Lindwall and that other fella." Pause
again. "Don't think they like me very much. Didn't really know
whether I ought to have coom back out 'ere again."

'Question: "What do you think of Arthur Morris now?"
Answer, after an immense silence: " 'Ave they got any sight-
screens yet down at the bottom end at Brisbane?" Long silence.
"Saw Arthur Morris make 196 once when the sight-screen had
blown down." Then he would lean forward, almost
confidentially, to one of the reporters and say: "Remember that,
Bill, the day when the sight-screens blew down?" and then he
would retreat into some extensive reverie of his own, while the
entire Australian press contingent sat transfixed by the
performance in total, respectful silence.'

Hutton's oblique style did not always serve him as well when it came to
dealing with awkward team issues later in the tour, but such was the
mutual respect between him and Trevor that Bailey always knew
where he stood. In Len's eyes, he could do little wrong.

The tour began with unprecedented victories over both Western
Australia and a Combined XI in Perth. Bailey did well enough in both
matches, bowling with life and accuracy, but suffered from a rash of
dropped catches close to the wicket. In the month or so before the first
Test in Brisbane, he secured his position as *the* all-rounder in the
England team by performance as well as reputation. The Brisbane
Test, lost by England, to the tune of an innings and 154 runs, brought
out the best in him, though there was one blot on his escutcheon.

It was a small one in the context of the errors made in the first place
by the selection of the team, which included four pace bowlers and no
spinner, and in the second place by Hutton's decision to put Australia
in to bat. Their total of 601 for 8 was made possible partly by a dozen or
so missed catches by England. Hutton described his feelings thus: 'And
when I watched the unbelievable when Bailey at long-leg missed
Morris [on 55] with a chance he would take ninety-nine times out of a
hundred, I began to feel there was a curse on the side.' Forgotten was

the fact that Bailey had split a finger in the previous match against Queensland and was fielding on the boundary for that reason.

Bad fielding, allied to an accident to Compton which meant he could hardly grip the bat and came in last in both England's innings, were misfortunes which England could well have done without. Bailey had the best bowling analysis in Australia's only innings – 3 wickets for 140 runs from twenty-six overs – but it was scarcely a match winning effort. He did, however, battle heroically: he went in to bat when England's answer to Australia's massive total had reached 26 for 4 wickets.

Bailey resisted for four hours and twenty minutes, adding 82 with Cowdrey and failing only when, with Compton a passenger as last man in, he went for the bowling and was out. It was not as if he was trying to break out of an entirely defensive mode. For, to those who did not know Trevor himself, but only his reputation for slow scoring, he had already produced a stroke of dazzling, unexpected cheek. Jumping out to Ian Johnson, Australia's captain and off-spinner, he wafted him for 6 runs over mid-wicket. An unusual occurrence of itself, it was made the more poignant by the fact that a local Queensland businessman had offered one hundred Australian pounds to the first Englishman to hit a six. As John Woodcock once wrote of the incident, 'Bailey was, you understand, nothing if not deliberate.' Trevor claims to this day that the hundred-pounds offer was far from the front of his mind. Deliberate or not, it was a lot of money in those days; quite enough for champagne to be bought to cool off in a couple of baths filled with ice in the team's Brisbane hotel, and for the England team to drown their sorrows after a humiliating defeat.

The first Test was a disaster for England in most respects, from the moment the team was selected. Hutton had already developed a hearty dislike for the Wagga ground at Brisbane before this match. Now his antipathy bordered on the paranoiac. His bowling had been thrashed, his fielders had shown a remarkable lack of alertness, his batsmen – Bailey, Cowdrey, Edrich and May apart – had failed. The fast attack on which he pinned his faith had not flourished. At the back of Hutton's mind throughout this tour, with his fine sense of history, and with the responsibility which pressed down on him so that caution became his watchword, was the thought that England had not won a series in Australia since 1933, when Jardine's men worked the oracle and nothing but controversy attended their efforts. Twenty-two years is a long time, even in a game like cricket, and England had a potentially well-balanced team. But they had not yet found an established opening partner for Hutton: Simpson had looked vulnerable and had made a string of low scores. Edrich had failed often but possessed the fighting qualities the captain so much admired. May, the vice-captain and crown prince to Hutton's throne, and Cowdrey, looked good. Bailey could be depended upon.

It was also in Hutton's mind that pace was the key to victory in Australia and that, in Tyson, he possessed a bowler, though raw and untried, who might blast out the Australians often enough to give England a chance. Brisbane had done nothing to strike fear into Australian hearts; quite the reverse. As all the world knows, Tyson's control was improved immensely by efforts made to cut down his run following the first Test and, in the end, it all came right. But it took a series of unplanned incidents and a certain amount of honest heartache to make it so.

The second match in the series at Sydney proved the turning-point after a sequence of events which began with the dropping of Alec Bedser and ended with Frank Tyson finding his real power as a fast bowler, after nearly losing his head to a Ray Lindwall bouncer. According to Trevor Bailey, the whole Bedser episode and what followed could have been entirely different: 'If Len had included Alec Bedser in the second Test at Sydney, which he probably should have done – because, in conditions favouring swing, Alec would have been more effective than anybody – we would have won that game more easily, but then would probably have lost the series.'

Bailey describes how, in that Sydney Test, England were put in to bat, and were then bowled out for 154. Without Bedser, and in conditions where the ability to swerve the ball in the air was the weapon most likely to produce wickets, Bailey found himself opening the bowling with Statham. He picked up 4 wickets for 59 in Australia's first innings, including the first three in the order. He feels, though, that

Bedser, who could swing the ball later and more effectively than anyone, would have taken 6 wickets at cheaper cost. Ironically, this would have left Bedser in the team for the third Test, depriving England of either Appleyard or Wardle. But the spinners were to play such a significant part not only in the series, but in the third Test at Melbourne, where they were responsible for irretrievably damaging Australia before Tyson tore them apart in the second innings.

The world is full of ifs and buts, but one thing is certain. Alec Bedser was deeply wounded, not only by the fact of his omission from the second Test. For, amongst all the happenings at Brisbane, his performance had been comparatively lack-lustre. He had to all intents and purposes recovered from the attack of shingles which had dogged him through the early part of the tour, but he had still been below his best. No, what hit Alec harder than his being dropped after carrying the burden of England's Test-match attack virtually since the war, was the manner of it. The first Alec knew of it was when he saw the team-sheet posted in the dressing-room just before the toss was made. As Trevor says: 'Len found it just impossible to have a quiet talk with Alec. He was very much aware of Alec's great service to England – especially when he had been the only real threat to Australia as well as the workhorse who bowled vast numbers of overs against them. He knew what his decision would mean to a great professional like Alec, and he couldn't bring himself to talk it over.'

Len Hutton himself has since deeply regretted the manner of Alec Bedser's going. His lugubrious words have the ring of melancholy truth:

'I hoped against hope that Alec might come to me and say:
"Look, I'm not 100 per cent fit, so don't consider me until I
am." But Alec was the type of fighter who would drag himself
on to the field to do his bit. His fitness was the prime concern of
both the tour committee and myself. I had noticed on the ship
that he was not his usual self and, within a day of his arrival in
Perth, he went down with shingles, a painful and debilitating
illness. A doctor told me that it would take weeks for him to be

105

right again, but he was so keen to get back, and I was so keen to have him back, that he played in three matches before the first Test and bowled well enough to make the Test team. I wish the doctor had been more decisive and flatly told me he was not to play for a defined period. Alec could have gone away and rested until he was fit.

'Another doubt had crept into my mind. George Duckworth, the scorer, drew my attention to the number of no-balls Alec bowled, which suggested he was untypically straining to get to the wicket. Also, although he was still a fine catcher in gully positions, he was rather slow in the field. I figured if he was rested at Sydney he would be refreshed and come back for the third match at Melbourne, but by then events had overtaken me and I certainly couldn't split the spearhead attack of Tyson and Statham.

'In mitigation, I had a lot of things on my mind before I pinned up the team-sheets, minus the name of Alec Bedser, in the dressing-rooms at Sydney and Melbourne, but I wish now I had talked with him and said: "Sorry, old mate, but you'll have to move over in the interests of the side. I know you'll be upset, but I'd like you to know that I'm upset too. I hate to have to do it." '

Hutton has also said that the making of Frank Tyson as an express, rather than just a very fast bowler, was being hit on the head by Lindwall in the second innings of that Sydney Test. He was never quite the same again – at least a yard quicker than he had ever been, even off his remoulded shorter run. Lindwall never bowled another bumper at Tyson and nor, it seems, did any other Australian. Tyson took 6 wickets in the second innings of that famous Sydney match, and 10 wickets in all. Australia had been set to score 223 for victory and failed by 38 runs. Bailey's part had been far from negligible. He had opened the innings without making much of a mark on the game with his batting, surviving for over half an hour in each innings, seeing off the new ball, but contributing little in the way of runs. His bowling had kept England in the game, however, paving the way for others – notably Tyson – to win it.

Through Tyson and Statham, England had reimposed the menace of speed on the Australian batsmen; but as Alan Ross of the *Observer* pointed out in his fine book, *Australia '55*, 'It had to be remembered that it was once again Bailey who started the fightback on the second day, when Australia were scoring at a rate enough to put any bowler out of composure. He performed the job that Bedser had so often done since the war on good wickets. He moved the ball consistently and sufficiently from a good length to reduce batsmen, hitherto scoring freely, to the defensive push that, like a virus, brings in train a whole lot of other symptoms.'

Before the third Test in Melbourne, Trevor was asked by Hutton to take Bedser to inspect the pitch, which was cracked but not necessarily menacing because of it. Whatever Bedser's views, he was once again left out of the team, and both Appleyard and Wardle were included. They took but 4 wickets between them in the two innings, but they were important ones. Once again, the chief damage was done by Tyson and Statham with respectively 9 and 7 wickets in the match.

The England batting contained two memorable innings: one, a century by Cowdrey in their first innings; the other, an imperious 91 by May in their second. Bailey had reverted to No. 6 in the order and contributed 54 runs for once out to England's victory by 128 runs. His second innings of 24 not out occupied nearly three hours while Evans and Wardle laid about them. Limited to three strokes – the forward defensive, the cut and the swing to leg – he favoured the forward defensive on a ratio of about a hundred to one. But England had been able to provide a further 106 runs while he was at the wicket. 'Firm in intent, unruffled by comment, and admirably devoted to the needs of his side,' is how Alan Ross described him at the end of that third Test.

It had been a Test of controversy. Australia had gained a lead of 40 runs in the first innings, their last 5 wickets adding 139 runs on the morning of the third day against expectation. The wicket, previously full of cracks, appeared to have been watered during the rest day on Sunday. The cracks disappeared, and batting became an altogether easier prospect as Len Maddocks, the Australian wicket-keeper, eased his side into what appeared to be a vital lead. England benefited just as much, however, from the changed nature of the pitch, and May's superb second innings left Australia with far too much to do in the face of Tyson and Statham. Tyson's fifth-day spell of 6 wickets for 16 runs hurtled out Australia in six and a half eight-ball overs in conditions which by then had again deteriorated.

The accusations of tampering with the wicket which ran throughout the Australian press were based as much on the need to prolong the game and swell gate receipts as on any skulduggery to make Australia's task easier. Firm denials were issued, reports by engineers produced to show that the changes were the result of natural causes; but no matter what, England's win had been conclusive – they had won by 128 runs in a low-scoring game with a day to spare and, from being one down in the series, they were now one up.

In those days, it was unusual for wives to be present on tour. Expense was one thing; distraction for the husband was often quoted as a further drawback. But even the lovely Greta Bailey had her limits. A month with Trevor, relatively frowned upon though this might be – though she had hardly seen him during the past twelve – did not seem too much to ask. Jean Evans and Dorothy Hutton were also in Australia, and a trend was set for the future. Of course, these days, the sky's the limit: wives, girlfriends, parents, lawyers, agents and minders are all on parade and often much in evidence. It would have taken more than the presence of a few wives to stop the momentum of Hutton's team in any case. (Not, I hasten to add, that their presence was not a positive bonus.) The fact was that England not only had the equipment, but the confidence to go forward. They had the batting to match Australia's, and they had a well-balanced attack, whatever the conditions. In Tyson, they had the fastest bowler in the world, at his peak.

Tyson, of course, owed much to Statham, especially, and to Bailey. For these were bowlers who could cause batsmen to fret; shackled at one end, they were more likely to fall prey to Tyson's fast ball of full length as they shaped to drive, only to find the ball through them before the bat came down. Tyson was the first to acknowledge how much he owed the chap at the other end.

And so to Adelaide. The lovely ground in the capital of South

Australia produced the best batting pitch of the series. Partly because of this, it was the only Test to be won by the side batting second, and it was the only Test in the series to be played over the full five days.

By now, the Australian cricket world, from the selectors down to the smallest member of the public, were in disarray. They were not used to the Poms playing the game harder than they did, playing to the letter without undue regard for the spirit of the laws, bowling faster and, worst of all, winning. There was controversy about the selection of the Australian team: three South Australians, Les Favell, Gil Langley and Graeme Hole, were omitted, although those who replaced them eventually justified themselves. Lindwall was unfit: a bitter blow.

England's tactics in the field during Australia's first innings did not endear them to the crowd, the Australian press, or the public. There had been mutterings about the deliberation with which England's fields were set, and the sluggishness of England's over rate, throughout the tour. Adelaide saw deterioration rather than improvement, and criticism continued unabated. It is possible to see why, quite apart from the fact that Australia were already down in the series by two matches to one. Hutton used his bowlers in short spells, no more than three or four overs at a time, and set his field on the occasion of each change with elaborate care. Even allowing for the intense heat, the rate of progress was tardy, and deliberately so in the eyes of the Australians. England's overall bowling rate in that Australian first innings was equivalent to thirteen six-ball overs an hour. This is something like the norm in modern Test cricket but, in those days, it was slow in the extreme. So, too, was Australia's batting for the most part. They did not wish to lose a war of attrition.

Bailey did more than his share in an Australian innings which reached 323 runs in 100 minutes short of two days. He took 3 for 39, among his wickets being the prolific Neil Harvey for 25: Harvey had consistently been Australia's most dangerous batsman. Bailey also broke the stand between Ian Johnson, Australia's captain, and Len Maddocks – both controversial choices – which had raised 92 for the ninth wicket.

Trevor did not bowl in the second innings, but he contributed hugely with the bat, in the now familiar way. He kept one end secure, seeing off the second new ball, while England's last five first-innings wickets added 109 precious runs. The reason he was not called upon for Australia's second innings was simple enough. After Appleyard had taken 3 early wickets, Statham and Tyson whisked out the next six Australian batsmen for 34 runs on the morning of the fifth day. 'Someone will pay for this,' Keith Miller is reputed to have said as he prepared to take the field for the England second innings; and England's notionally simple task of scoring 97 runs to win the match and retain the Ashes suddenly took on a Herculean aspect as Miller dismissed Hutton, Edrich and Cowdrey for 18 runs and then took a brilliant catch to get rid of May with only 49 on the board. Bailey, however, in partnership with Compton, proved yet again the rock on which Australia foundered. He stayed until the match, and the series, were almost won.

The fifth Test at Sydney was drastically cut by rain. Only three days' play were possible, but Bailey rounded off a fine series with one last gesture. Though by no means in a crisis, he contrived to spend nearly three hours over a half-century in England's only innings – just to remind them, so to say. And then, as if to tantalise the Australians still further, he took the attack apart with a series of lofted drives off everyone. The great Raymond Lindwall, especially, felt the force of his bat. But, needing only one wicket to achieve 100 in Test matches against England, Lindwall was bowling what could have been his last over against England when Bailey surrendered his wicket to him, in the nicest possible way, congratulated him and walked off the field with 72 runs against his name. If there could be such a brief summary of what made Trevor Bailey tick, it was that innings.

Bailey's contribution to England's victory in 1954–55, though sometimes overshadowed by the fast bowling of Tyson and Statham, and by the batting of the emergent May and Cowdrey, had been scarcely less significant than the part he had played in the regaining of the Ashes in 1953. There have been few finer moments in Test cricket than in the cut and thrust of his duels with the magnificent and flamboyant Keith Miller throughout the series. Two fine all-rounders, cast in entirely different moulds, they had served their sides splendidly in their own ways. Sparks flew visibly when they confronted each other, especially when Miller had the ball. Nobody appreciated Bailey's worth more than Miller, and for that reason he seemed incensed with the need to destroy that infuriating imperturbability displayed by Bailey whenever they met.

Bailey had celebrated his thirty-second birthday in Australia. You are in your prime as a batsman at thirty-two, they say; but past the pink of any fast bowler's performance. Yet he modelled himself on his limitations so well that Alan Ross could say '. . . as a bowler [he] largely ignored the stumps, but he moved the ball more than any bowler in either side, and his skill in floating his slower ball across the wicket in both directions got him important wickets, particularly Harvey's.' His 10 wickets in the series were thus of immense value. The worth of his batting may be gauged by his 296 runs for an average of 37 on wickets not always of the highest quality. Once again, the Australians had brought the best out of Bailey.

There was little for him to do in New Zealand during the short series at the end of a five-month tour. Tyson and Statham continued to sweep all before them, and Appleyard came even more into his own. New Zealand were nowhere as strong as they had been in 1949, say, and there were easy pickings. The home team were bowled out for 26 in the second and final Test match: Statham 3 for 9, Tyson 2 for 10, Appleyard 4 for 7. Bailey did not bowl.

Apart from his invaluable contributions on the field in the five months or so since the MCC team had left England, Trevor had established a reputation among the party as a sort of seasoned, avuncular figure, with a broad entrepreneurial streak and a word of sound advice on most subjects under the sun. His ability to learn from experience was not only an asset on the cricket field. Who better to consult than Frank Tyson, hero of that particular tour? 'Trevor was infinitely kind to junior players. He it was who guided me through the shoals of cricket business by introducing me to his agent, the late Bagenal Harvey. When we returned to England via America in 1954–55, he chaperoned the younger element of the team around the States, taking them to shows and to Eddie Condon's night-club and

111

introducing them to the hospitality of his millionaire friend, the late Henry Sayens.'

But, by this time, Trevor was on his way back to even more business than usual. He was appointed secretary of Essex before the beginning of the 1955 season. This gave him precious little time for relaxation during the month or so before he was playing cricket again. Besides, the South Africans had landed.

6

The Middle Years

1955–58

The South African touring party of 1955 contained a number of those who had gone to Australia in 1953 and, with a team under Jack Cheetham which was given no chance at all, had succeeded in drawing the series. Their fielding, then, had stretched the art of catching and run-saving beyond standards previously thought possible. They had demonstrated that no cause was so lost as to be irredeemable. They were a fighting force based on high-class defensive qualities in the field. Now, in 1955, many of those qualities remained. Cheetham's team in England took time to find their feet but, having lost the first two Test matches, they went to the Oval for the final match all-square.

While England had a good all-round team, South Africa almost matched them man for man. They had in Jack McGlew a batsman of truly adhesive qualities and, in Roy McLean and Paul Winslow, two fine, upstanding strikers of the ball who could take apart any attack. Bailey's opposite number in the all-rounder stakes was Trevor Goddard, a defensive bowler of immense accuracy to rival Bailey's but bowling left-arm at medium-pace. In a series which also saw the full rehabilitation of Denis Compton on the international scene came confirmation of May's status as one of the great batsmen the game has produced.

Yet it was something of a transitional time for England: no Hutton, no Edrich, little Bedser, little Appleyard, and a new captain in Peter May. They just scraped home in the series, winning by three matches to two. They found in Hugh Tayfield, the South African off-spinner, a bowler of uncanny guile and accuracy; and, supported by superb fielding, Tayfield and Goddard, with a largely leg-stump attack, tied

113

down England, made them tug against the collar. Peter Heine and Neil Adcock proved no mean answer to the all-conquering Tyson and Statham. So there was little in it at the end.

Bailey played in all five Tests. His penchant for taking on all comers was seen to best advantage in the third Test at Old Trafford, when he scored 44 in the first innings, adding 144 with Compton for the fifth wicket, and defended stubbornly in the second in an attempt to deny South Africa time in which to complete victory. In all, he batted for almost six hours in the match, scored 82 runs for once out, and bowled thirty-seven overs in South Africa's first innings.

South Africa won this match by 3 wickets with only a few minutes to spare. They also won the fourth Test, despite Bailey's resistance for two hours at the death. In that time, having gone in at the fall of the fourth wicket, he mustered 8 runs. He was last out, with two hours of the final day remaining, and South Africa had at last won a Test match at Headingley, despite the adversity of injury to Adcock and the loss of their first 7 wickets for 98 runs on the first day. Directing his attack for the most part on or around the leg stump, Bailey bowled more than fifty-six overs in the match and took 4 wickets for 120 runs.

The final match at the Oval saw England take the series. The South Africans were edged out of the game by 92 runs thanks to Laker and Lock, on their own midden, taking 15 wickets between them. It was not Trevor Bailey's finest hour – he took 1 wicket and scored 1 run in the match – but if he had, for him, an indifferent series, his season overall ranked high by contemporary standards. Altogether, he took 89 wickets in a good summer for batsmen and scored nearly 1,500 runs.

It was not a vintage year, though. He had been playing cricket virtually non-stop for nearly three years by the end of it. His strike rate was a wicket every ten overs. He was scoring his runs less quickly even in county cricket, finding it more difficult to get out of the defensive groove. He was undefeated in nearly a quarter of the innings he played that summer, which could have argued that intense concentration had taken over from the urge to accelerate, no matter how slowly. He was thirty-three now, and he was tired, by his standards anyway.

There were several bright spots: 152 not out against Kent at Clacton, together with 7 wickets for 105 runs in the match; 54 and 114 not out (100 of them before lunch) and a haul of 5 for 68 against Nottinghamshire at Southend; and he had joy against the South Africans at Colchester, saving the game and forming a partnership of 184 with Doug Insole, making 107 himself.

Playing in that Essex versus South Africa game – it was one of my four appearances for the county that season – I was conscious of several things. Among them was the way Trevor prepared for an innings: the corset, the sticking plaster round the fingers, the chewing gum, neatly marshalled and laid out, the splash of cold water in the face just before going out to bat – hatless, just one thigh guard in those days, even with Adcock and Heine bouncing the ball around on a true but fast pitch. Then there was the elaborate trouble he took over marking his guard, grooving the ground with his bat and his spikes with such unmistakable care that it was as if he was locking himself in for the day.

The game took place shortly before the first Test, and he was keen to lodge a reminder. He succeeded admirably with the bat, scoring run for run with his old friend Insole while they both made centuries. With the ball he was less successful. Both he and I bowled more overs than anyone else while the South Africans compiled 503 for 4 wickets in their only innings. We each conceded more than 100 runs, each bowled thirty-two overs although, while there was a lot of stick flying around on a beautiful wicket, it was all comparatively peaceful until Roy McLean came in. He made his undefeated century in less than two hours, and there was nothing anyone, not even Trevor with all his guile and experience, could do about it.

I found myself fielding at long-off to Trevor, my walk in starting from the boundary boards. Ray Smith was at deep extra-cover. Trevor bowled. Neither of us moved more than a yard or two before the ball smashed against the fence between us; not once but three times in that over. It was a measure of Trevor's resilience that he should go out and score a hundred after what can only be described as a severe mauling. It assured his place in the Test team, but there can be no doubt that he had earned a winter's rest from playing cricket by the end of that season.

There was plenty to do, anyway. Looking after Essex's affairs as their secretary was one thing, fulfilling various engagements arranged for him by Bagenal Harvey, his agent, was another. Then there was the opportunity of getting to know his first two children, Kim and the recently arrived Justin, before the new season and Ian Johnson's 1956 Australian team arrived upon the scene. It was Jim Laker's benefit year. With immaculate timing, the rains came, and Laker was in his element. When somebody takes all 10 wickets in an innings twice in a season – both times against the Australians – and when, in a *Test*, he nearly takes 20 in the match, there is little room for anyone else. Laker's feats captured the public's imagination to such an extent that little else was cricket news. But there was a lot going on out there besides Jim Laker's sorcery.

Like a number of others, Trevor Bailey was an interested and admiring onlooker when England were in the field against Australia. Before that, however, he seized the opportunity to make his mark on the series. Significantly, it was at Lord's, his happy hunting-ground from way back, and the Australians' home from home. Equally significantly, it was on the only occasion when England had the worst of it that Bailey shone.

The first Test at Nottingham had been drawn, but with the odds weighted heavily in England's favour. Bailey bowled only twelve overs in the match: Lock, Laker and Appleyard took all thirteen Australian wickets to fall. Batting at No. 6 while the young Peter Richardson and Colin Cowdrey formed a successful opening partnership, Bailey had no crisis to overcome and made 14 in his only innings. At Lord's, however, he played two long, defiant innings, sharing fruitful partnerships with Peter May on both occasions. He also picked up 6 good wickets in the match. But England's cause was rendered a lost one by Keith Miller, who in his thirty-seventh year took 10 wickets in the match, his last at Lord's at this level. He threw the bails to the crowd as he walked off at the end of England's second innings, and they rose to him. Lord's on the big occasion brought the best out of him as it did Bailey, his great rival and (on the surface, anyway) *bête noire*.

The third Test at Leeds gave Bailey the chance to renew

116

acquaintance with another of the scenes of his former triumphs against Australia. His undefeated 33 in two and a quarter hours, after going in at the fall of the sixth wicket, enabled England to make 325 from 248 for 7: enough to beat Australia by an innings. Lock and Laker took 18 wickets between them, and the seam and swing of Trueman and Bailey was rendered virtually surplus to requirements. As for the fourth Test at Manchester, it was all Laker: the Ashes were duly retained. And a slight injury before the fifth Test gave the selectors the chance to play their options without committing themselves to dropping the man whom everybody – if they bothered to think about it all – was considered England's number one, if not their only real, all-rounder.

This was an interesting and crucial time in Trevor's career: towards the end of the middle game, so to speak. The cricket world itself was at a crossroads. The public were beginning to find the defensive pattern into which the game had fallen somewhat irksome; and they were beginning to vote with their feet. As the arch-priest of defensive batting and, to some extent, bowling, Bailey was beginning to move into the sights of one or two snipers in powerful positions. Legislation was already under way to limit the number of fielders on the leg side in domestic cricket: five was to become the limit, with no more than two behind the batsman on that side of the wicket. It came into play in 1957 and was a sure sign that people were concerned for the game at large, and not just the winning and losing of it. Not that this was a real threat yet to the likes of Trevor. But the time was to come, not too far hence, when Boycott and Barrington were dropped from the England team for making large scores too slowly.

His absence from the fifth Test against Australia notwithstanding, Trevor was among the first of those picked for the winter tour of South Africa. It would have been unthinkable for MCC to go without him, although in fact they almost did. Trevor had accepted the kind offer of a friend to drive him to Waterloo to catch the boat train to Southampton, only to find the road from Southend lined with commuter traffic. Even the cool, unruffled exterior of the great Essex all-rounder was shattered when he found that the boat train had left without him. Alternative arrangements were hastily made, and it was a greatly fussed but none the less relieved Bailey who hastened up the gangway to join his team-mates on the boat for Cape Town.

Trevor had good reason not to want to miss the boat, quite apart from the cricketing aspects. He had been commissioned to line up the sale of a certain amount of electrical switch-gear during his safari round South Africa. Another factor was that he was looking forward to touring for the first, and what was to be the only, time with his great friend and Essex colleague, Doug Insole. Since Brian Taylor, the Essex wicket-keeper, was also a member of the MCC party, it was in those days a unique event. Never before had Essex provided three members of a touring team, and the occasion had been swiftly marked by a special dinner given in honour of the trio at the behest of the Essex president, Hubert Ashton.

The boat trip to South Africa was a wonderful experience. Not as seemingly timeless as the journey to Australia, it was just the right length, superbly luxurious, with no time for spells of boredom, but time enough for fun and games and the making of a firm team spirit. Contemplating Table Mountain at dawn, shrouded in its cloth of cloud, Trevor could reflect on a good season behind him. It was not a special one in terms of taking wickets – he had taken 78 at 21.75 apiece – but a good one with the bat: he had finished third in the first-class averages with a total of 1,186 runs, his average of nearly 44 being boosted by an extraordinary eleven undefeated innings in thirty-eight visits to the crease.

What he was assuredly not contemplating was a series of five Test matches in which he was to open the innings in every one, alongside Peter Richardson. Spending his time on the boat keeping fit; playing his own notorious, but sometimes effective, hand of Bailey bridge; counterbalancing all those deck games by attending various parties; reading, among other things, Nicholas Monsarrat's *Tribe that lost its Head*, which he was later to discover he could not take into South Africa, he saw no further than batting in the middle order and acting as third seamer to two of the three fast bowlers, Tyson, Statham and Loader.

There had been no tour of South Africa by MCC since 1948–49, and it was a new experience for everyone making the visit, except Denis

Compton and Godfrey Evans. The players were genuinely concerned about the various aspects of apartheid. As Bailey says, as cricketers, they were apolitical but unable to shut their eyes to a situation in which there appeared to be no satisfactory solution for all the different racial and religious groups involved. They were aware, too, even then, that it was not a clear-cut, black-versus-white dilemma with which the country was faced.

It was Peter May's first tour as captain. Doug Insole, his vice-captain, had not toured before. Trevor, though not the most experienced player, naturally fell into the position of wise-man and guru, but was as unaware as anyone of the responsibility that was to be thrust upon him. The 1956 Australian series had seen Richardson and Cowdrey open the batting for England with success, and it was naturally assumed that, failing a complete loss of form by either one, the partnership would continue. In the event, Cowdrey and Richardson did reasonably well in the preliminary games during the two months prior to the first Test in Johannesburg. (It is interesting to note that MCC had been in South Africa two months almost to the day when the first Test started, when that is compared with the hustle and bustle of current tours abroad.) But the fact was that Cowdrey expressed a wish not to open; the other opener, Alan Oakman, had not made the grade; and, looking around, the eye naturally alighted on 'Mr Stop-gap' himself. It turned out to be a series made for the specialised brand of do-or-die cricket at which Trevor so excelled.

Being asked to open the innings in Johannesburg only a short time before the start of play was just the thing to put Trevor on his mettle. It was not long before the schoolboyish sense of humour typical of both these very good players surfaced. Neither Richardson nor Bailey would claim to be anything but honest artisans in the trade of opening the batting for England. A strictly limited range of strokes, a short back-lift, an eye for the quick single, concentration, and seemingly infinite patience were what they had in common. One left-handed, the other right, they were there to grind it out against a predominantly leg-stump attack, and grind it out they did.

It was a series of slow scoring against accurate bowling and often

119

brilliant catching and ground fielding, although nothing surpassed the slowness of tempo developed in England's first innings of the series. Bailey made 16 out of England's 45 for 2 scored in the 140 minutes before lunch. During the opening partnership of 28, and before the first Test-match crowd to number 100,000 people, the air was rent with cries of 'Come one, Sir Jack'. Or, 'Not now, Herbert'. The South African fielders were nonplussed. It was some time before they realised that Bailey was Jack Hobbs, Richardson Herbert Sutcliffe, and irony was the order of the day.

'Herbert' went on to score the slowest century to that date recorded in Test cricket. Altogether, he scored 117 runs in fourteen minutes short of nine hours. It proved to be a match-winning innings. For Bailey seized on the opportunity afforded by Frank Tyson developing overnight tonsillitis, after South Africa had responded with 91 for 1 wicket; he shrugged off the mantle of Jack Hobbs and became once more the thinking man's fast-medium bowler, attacking the South Africans, forcing them into mistakes. His 3 wickets for 33 runs in the first innings were followed by 5 for 20 as South Africa were tumbled out for 72, and England won by the handsome margin of 131 runs. He also found time during that first innings to take a slip catch, coming forward and to his right to a lightning snick from Clive van Ryneveld off Statham's bowling which, because of the anticipation as well as the execution involved, he rates as one of his best ever.

For Bailey, it was to be a triumphant series and a tour which did nothing but enhance his reputation. He and Richardson put on over 70 in each innings before being separated in the second Test at Cape Town, a match also won by England after the South Africans had been utterly bamboozled by Wardle's left-arm china-men and googlies. In the third Test at Durban, the opening partnership had a hundred on the board before lunch, and Bailey made 80 out of England's first-innings 218. In the second innings, he suffered a cracked bone in the back of his right hand as a result of a Heine bouncer. He batted to the end of that day but did not resume until England were wobbling at 167 for 5; in a situation made for him, he stayed for fifty-five minutes with his hands in plaster while Doug Insole moved towards a century which, in the end, cost South Africa their chance of victory in what became a drawn match. Bailey was out to a poor decision, having been caught off his pads without benefit of bat.

Two up and two to play was a happy position for England when they returned to Johannesburg, but they failed to make the most of it. Nor did fortune, in the shape of some ghastly umpiring decisions – not just bad, but woefully inept – smile on them. 'Don't malign Malan: he's doing the best he can,' had become a bitter saying in the England camp during the Durban Test as one doubtful decision followed another. Umpire Malan either practised a form of injustice which would have done credit to the infamous South African Prime Minister of that name, or simply had a bad match. It depends upon whom you talk to about it.

Bailey's 5 wickets for 66 in the fourth Test was the best return of any England bowler. He batted with his customary aplomb without making many runs; only one in the second innings, which ended in circumstances which contained a touch of *déjà vu* and must have seemed like a bad dream. Later, Doug Insole used to tell the story on rainy days in Essex.

'Well,' he would say, 'the old Boil, you have to remember, had received a dodgy decision at the hands of Mr Malan at Durban, as the ball lobbed off his pad to short-leg where it was taken by Clive van Ryneveld. The trouble was, the Boil hadn't hit it. Once bitten, twice shy. So when it comes to the last over of the fourth day at Jo'burg, the game nicely in the balance, and no one keener than the Boil that England should not lose a wicket, he is facing "Toey" Tayfield, bowling over the wicket at the leg stump. The Boil shoves his left pad down the wicket so far that he is almost treading on Tayfield's foot. No chance of an lbw; but so as to make sure, the Boil removes his bat from the firing line, taking it well away from everything. The ball lobs off his pad to short-leg, some idiot shouts, "Catch it." Russell Endean does, but with no intention of claiming a catch. But there's Basil Malan with his finger up high enough for the bloke in the back row of the highest stand at the Wanderers ground to see it, and there's the Boil standing still as a statue, bat aloft, left dog down the track, a study in immobility. It is the last ball of the day. The umpires take off the bails, Peter

Richardson and the South African team leave the field, the crowd melts away. Then out come the groundstaff with their brooms to sweep the ends and tidy up before it gets dark. As we're leaving our showers and drying off, someone looks out of the window. "My God, he's still there," he exclaims. And there he was, the old boy, shaking his head slowly, looking at his pad, then his bat, then both of them together. It wasn't so much dissent, just a silent protest.'

This description, Trevor insists, is grossly exaggerated. But he does admit to being unhappy. Nor has distance to the event lent any touch of enchantment, for England lost the match by only 17 runs.

Nothing brought the best out of Bailey like adversity, and the fifth and final Test at Port Elizabeth saw him play a great innings on a deeply unreliable pitch. The ball often shot through inches off the ground, and Evans, keeping wicket to Tyson in the second innings, defied all convention by standing neither up nor back so that he could take the shooter before it bounced twice, though the ball that came through normally put him at high risk. It was one of the finest, if most unorthodox, exhibitions of wicket-keeping that Trevor has ever seen.

South Africa won the match because they won the toss. Their 164 in the first innings was the highest total of the match. Bailey had 3 wickets for 23 runs from twenty-five overs, which says something about the pitch. Then he went in and scored 41 runs out of England's 110 all out. Bailey's front-foot technique was made for these conditions. He stood yards out of his ground even to Adcock and Heine, then two of the fastest bowlers in the world, in a successful attempt to upset them. Anything of a full length he drove with a straight bat. He and Peter May added 54 runs for the third wicket before May was out. Bailey survived for two hours and twenty-five minutes in all, and he scored nearly half the runs made from the bat. But despite this, and although Tyson at last came into his own on this tour with a devastating 6 for 40, England went down by 58 runs, and the rubber was squared.

Taking into account all the matches played on that tour, Bailey's all-round record in South Africa was his best, anywhere, any time. In Test matches alone, he scaled even greater heights: fourth in the batting averages, ahead of May and Compton; top of the bowling.

There is no record of his achievements in the world of promoting sales of electrical equipment, but the chances are he did a first-class job. Those who had doubted his worth during the summer of 1956 were confounded. It was to be many moons before he could be written off.

Quite apart from his success as a player, Bailey had impressed the South Africans, players and cricket followers alike, with his fighting qualities. He had also made an indelible impact on an opposition who sometimes, in their keenness, and through ignorance rather than malice aforethought, tended to be rather too flexible when it came to interpreting the laws of the game. It was not exactly that, but more of a misunderstanding of the agreed position, which led to an interesting, not to say extraordinary scene, at Pretoria on 10th December 1956. It was the end of the third day of the match against a South African XI. It was three games before the first Test, played on a thoroughly unsuitable pitch, in the heart of Afrikanerdom, and MCC had needed to score 148 to win. It meant scoring more runs in an innings than either side had previously mustered.

Coming in at 21 for 4, Bailey stayed more than four hours for 26 runs. He was batting with Tony Lock, and the two of them kept the South Africans at bay until the scheduled close of play at 6:30 p.m. To Trevor's astonishment, McGlew, the opposition captain, then went rushing off the field while everyone else stood around waiting. Bailey politely enquired what was going on and was told that McGlew had gone off to see Insole, captaining MCC in that match, about claiming the extra half-hour. For a man who had batted for four hours to see out the day, this was too much. 'What, without informing the batsmen?', he asked incredulously. 'Come on, Tony,' were his next words, and he and Lock, who needed no urging, marched off to the England dressing-room, leaving umpires and fielders agog . . .

It turned out that communication over the playing conditions had been at fault, and Trevor had to return, reluctant but dignified to the end. He later admitted he had made a fatal mistake. 'I should,' he said, 'have got into the shower straightaway.'

Yet, like all who have toured South Africa with MCC, he found the hospitality and warmth of the cricketing fraternity off the field

123

overwhelming in its sincere desire to make the tour an enjoyable experience. And enjoy himself he did, in those days when the world was a simpler if less just place. The whole wide scope and wild beauty of the country and its animals impressed him deeply. When Greta joined him for a holiday at the end of the tour, having flown from Southend Airport with Penny Cowdrey over three days and nights, they stayed with friends, Reg Taylor and his wife. Reg came from Southend and was a former Essex player. Sharon, Trevor's daughter, born as a result of those happy days, is, as he says, 'a continual reminder of that holiday'. In the same way, Christopher Cowdrey, born a day earlier than Sharon, has been a cricketer whose career Trevor has followed with more than usual interest.

The year that had begun so well for him in South Africa continued its prosperous course throughout the 1957 domestic season. He played in four of the five Test matches against West Indies and had a marvellous match for England against them at Lord's.

The taming of Ramadhin and Valentine was the real story of England's success in the Test series by three matches to none. The supremacy of England's batting – May, Richardson, Cowdrey and Graveney were all hungry for runs and sated themselves – was established in the first Test at Nottingham, when May and Cowdrey showed Ramadhin that they had his measure by adding 411 for England's fourth wicket. But that match was drawn, and it was Bailey who established the bridgehead in the Lord's Test which enabled England to sweep all before them as the series progressed. This time it was his bowling that did England proud. It was a lively pitch whereon West Indies, having won the toss, chose to bat with some misgiving. When Trueman yorked Asgarali for 0 with 7 on the board, it seemed likely that he and Statham, at the other end, would be the chief danger, and Bailey would merely be useful in his supporting role.

This time, however, Trevor's accuracy and movement off the seam at his lively fast-medium pace proved tailor-made for the circumstances. It was his fiftieth Test match – and doubtless he was even keener than usual to give the public something to remember him by.

England v West Indies. Second Test at Lord's. June 20, 21, 22, 1957

West Indies

N. Asgarali lbw b Trueman	0	— c Trueman b Wardle	26
Rohan Kanhai c Cowdrey b Bailey	34	— c Bailey b Statham	0
C. L. Walcott lbw b Bailey	14	— c Trueman b Bailey	21
G. Sobers c May b Statham	17	— c May b Bailey	66
E. D. Weekes c Evans b Bailey	13	— c Evans b Bailey	90
F. M. Worrell c Close b Bailey	12	— c Evans b Trueman	10
O. G. Smith c Graveney b Bailey	25	— lbw b Statham	5
J. D. Goddard c Cowdrey b Bailey	1	— c Evans b Trueman	21
S. Ramadhin b Trueman	0	— c Statham b Bailey	0
R. Gilchrist c and b Bailey	4	— not out	11
A. L. Valentine not out	0	— b Statham	1
B 2, 1-b 1, w 4	7	B 4, 1-b 6	10

1/7 2/34 3/55 4/79 5/85 6/118 7/120   127
8/123 9/127

1/0 2/17 3/32 4/80 5/180   261
6/203 7/233 8/241 9/256

England

P. E. Richardson b Gilchrist	76
D. V. Smith lbw b Worrell	8
T. W. Graveney lbw b Gilchrist	0
P. B. H. May c Kanhai b Gilchrist	0
M. C. Cowdrey c Walcott b Sobers	152
T. E. Bailey b Worrell	1
D. B. Close c Kanhai b Goddard	32
T. G. Evans b Sobers	82

J. H. Wardle c Sobers b Ramadhin ... 11
F. S. Trueman not out 36
J. B. Statham b Gilchrist 7
B 7, 1-b 11, w 1 19

1/25 2/34 3/34 4/129 5/134   —
6/192 7/366 8/379 9/387   424

England Bowling

	O.	M.	R.	W.	O.	M.	R.	W.
Statham	18	3	46	1	29.1	9	71	3
Trueman	12.3	2	30	2	23	5	73	2
Bailey	21	8	44	7	22	6	54	4
Wardle					22	5	53	1

West Indies Bowling

	O.	M.	R.	W.
Worrell	42	7	114	2
Gilchrist	36.3	7	115	4
Ramadhin	22	5	83	1
Valentine	3	0	20	0
Goddard	13	1	45	1
Sobers	7	0	28	2

Umpires: D. Davies and C. S. Elliott.

Rohan Kanhai, unusually pressed into opening the batting, and Clyde Walcott had taken the score to 34, when Bailey brought one back to Walcott and had him leg before; the slide was on. The young Gary Sobers fell to Statham with the score on 55, but then Trevor completed as handsome a treble as he has ever had by removing Weekes and Worrell; and with the three Ws under his belt, he then accounted for Collie Smith, John Goddard and Roy Gilchrist. He finished with 7 wickets for 44 runs in twenty-one overs. West Indies were all out for 127 in less than four hours, and they were beyond recovery.

Facing England's 424, West Indies were well served in their second innings by Weekes and by Sobers. Weekes's 90, made despite a broken finger, was one of the great Test-match innings, and the twenty-year-old Sobers gave a taste of riches to come. But Bailey had them both caught behind the wicket, having already accounted for Walcott, and he finished with 4 for 54, which gave him figures of 11 for 98 in the match. His fiftieth Test match was certainly one to remember.

Bailey was forced to drop out of the fourth Test at Leeds and strangely finished with the startling batting average of 1.66 from the Test matches in which he did play. But the series was no real contest after that Lord's match.

Loudly though he was applauded by the Lord's crowd on that June Saturday when the match was over with two days to spare – even though they had been deprived of a full day's cricket – another, earlier coup of the 1957 season had given him no less pleasure. On that occasion, he was given a warm ovation by friend and foe alike which lasted from the moment the match ended until his back had disappeared from sight into the pavilion. Essex had just beaten Hampshire at Romford by 46 runs. Brian Taylor had caught Hampshire's last man, Malcolm Heath, off Trevor's bowling and had thus put the finishing touch to a quite remarkable *tour de force*. Trevor's performance in that match was one of the great all-round achievements in the first-class game of that or any other season, and proved that drama and bravura performance were at the centre of his cricketing life.

At this stage of the season, Essex v Hampshire was a run-of-the-mill, midweek county match at the sometimes appropriately named Gallows

126

Corner ground. Romford Cricket Club could generally be relied upon for a good batting wicket. That day, Saturday 25th May, it was a little on the green side, admirably suited to that formidable Hampshire trio, Derek Shackleton, Vic Cannings and the giant Malcolm Heath.

Ron Evans, an amateur from the Ilford club, was beaten and bowled all over the place by a typically late in-swinger from Shackleton, and Gordon Barker, the other Essex opener, was lbw to Cannings; only 9 runs were on the board. Bailey came in at the fall of the third wicket, that of Doug Insole, his captain. By that time, Essex had mustered 40 runs, and Brian 'Tonker' Taylor had mixed a few juicy blows with a number of snicks on both sides of his left-hander's wicket. The morning was an hour old when Bailey settled in carefully. The two of them added 47 runs before Heath removed Taylor on the stroke of lunch, and the general opinion was that, at 90 for 4, Essex had not had too bad a morning. It was the sort of score they were used to digesting along with the local caterer's cold ham and chocolate gateau.

The afternoon was a benefit for Hampshire's bowlers, spoiled only by Bailey's forward defensive movement, interlaced by the occasional crisp drive or square cut. A lifter from Heath hit him a painful blow on the right hand, but that was the only 'success' Hampshire had against him as, virtually alone, he resisted and plundered. Essex had lost 5 afternoon wickets for 40 runs and he had made 27 of these, 59 in all, when, with the last man in, he drove ambitiously at Heath and was bowled. The Essex total of 130 had been made in the face of some tidy and characteristically parsimonious Hampshire bowling and Heath, with his ability to obtain extra bounce from the wicket, had taken 4 for 37 off twenty-four overs.

Unbuckling his pads, removing his thigh-pad, bolstered by a towel, and glancing anxiously at the swelling surrounding a knuckle on his right hand which later proved to be cracked, Trevor took the field, limbered up, opened the bowling and, after one slash for four by Roy Marshall, began to make inroads. In his first half-dozen overs, he bowled Marshall with a classic out-swinger and brought one back to have Jimmy Gray leg before. Only 8 Hampshire runs were on the board. Although Bailey sought medical attention for his hand during

127

the day, and although Colin Ingleby-Mackenzie and Mike Barnard put on 45 for the fifth wicket, Trevor returned on the Monday morning to sweep away the last four Hampshire wickets while 27 were scored. He finished with 6 wickets for 32 runs from seventeen overs, and looked forward to putting his feet up for a bit after checking how things were around the ground and in the mobile Essex office.

He was scarcely back in the dressing-room before he was scuttling round for pads and other accoutrements, all thoughts of secretarial duties out of the window. Shackleton and Cannings, names as familiar on the county circuit as Marks and Spencer, were at work and, within a couple of overs of the start of the Essex second innings, had taken the wickets of Barker, Evans and Insole. When Bailey went out to bat, the scoreboard showed the loss of three wickets for no runs – not even an extra – and it was a case of 'here we go again'. No other batsman reached the 20s, and only three made double figures while Bailey took on the Hampshire attack once more. He made 71 before running out of partners, scoring most freely, but not with consistent freedom, against Heath. He farmed the bowling as well as he could, scoring half his side's runs and remaining undefeated to the end, putting on 29 precious runs for the last wicket with Ian King, who made only 9 but was happy to have played a part in Essex's final total of 141.

The pitch was never going to belong to the batsmen, but the making of 163 runs to win was certainly on Hampshire's agenda. Ten minutes between innings, and then Bailey was measuring out his run and setting his field: three slips and a gully, two short-legs, a third-man, two men saving one. Only Jimmy Gray, a man of solid worth and a grafter and, the following day, the young Colin Ingleby-Mackenzie withstood him. A man of incredible reserves, Bailey called upon them all. His first spell brought him the wickets of Marshall and the stolid Henry Horton. Refreshed overnight, there was no holding him. Barnard and Ingleby-Mackenzie, the only men to reach double figures in company with Gray, both fell to him as he moved the ball both ways off the seam to a full length. He whisked the tail aside. Then Gray, too, after compiling a brave 40, fell to a catch in the gully. When Malcolm Heath was caught at the wicket and a stentorian appeal from Brian Taylor split the

Essex v Hampshire at Romford. May 25, 27, 28 1957

Essex

G. Barker lbw b Cannings	5	— b Shackleton	0
R. E. Evans b Shackleton	4	— b Cannings	0
B. Taylor lbw b Heath	35	— run out	17
D. J. Insole b Heath	14	— b Shackleton	0
T. E. Bailey b Heath	59	— not out	71
M. Bear b Cannings	2	— c Sainsbury b Shackleton	1
G. Smith c Harrison b Shackleton	5	— lbw b Shackleton	4
A. Durley b Heath	4	— c Eagar b Cannings	11
R. Ralph b Sainsbury	1	— b Sainsbury	16
K. C. Preston b Sainsbury	1	— b Shackleton	0
I. M. King not out	0	— c Eagar b Heath	9
		B 5, 1-b 7	12

1/9 2/9 3/40 4/87 5/94 6/105 7/117   130
8/118 9/120

1/0 2/0 3/0 4/38 5/44   141
6/48 7/75 8/105 9/112

Hampshire

R. E. Marshall b Bailey	4	— c Taylor b Bailey	6
J. R. Gray lbw b Bailey	2	— c King b Bailey	40
H. Horton run out	1	— c Taylor b Bailey	7
P. J. Sainsbury b Ralph	5	— lbw b Preston	3
H. M. Barnard c King b Insole	26	— b Bailey	15
A. C. D. Ingleby-Mackenzie not out	37	— c Taylor b Bailey	23
L. Harrison b Insole	8	— b Bailey	5
E. D. R. Eagar c Taylor b Bailey	0	— c Insole b King	3
D. Shackleton lbw b Bailey	5	— not out	7
V. H. D. Cannings b Bailey	7	— b Bailey	2
M. Heath c Insole b Bailey	0	— c Taylor b Bailey	0
B 4, 1-b 10	14	B 4, 1-b 1	5

1/5 2/8 3/9 4/27 5/72 6/82 7/83   109
8/89 9/109

1/6 2/26 3/34 4/62 5/95   116
6/100 7/103 8/103 9/116

Hampshire Bowling

	O.	M.	R.	W.		O.	M.	R.	W.
Shackleton	16	6	37	2	....	26	6	47	5
Cannings	16	10	15	2	....	27	14	30	2
Sainsbury	24	10	41	2	....	4	3	4	1
Heath	24.2	9	37	4	....	18.4	1	48	1

Essex Bowling

	O.	M.	R.	W.		O.	M.	R.	W.
Bailey	17	5	32	6	....	23	7	49	8
Preston	14	5	30	0	....	17.5	6	31	1
Ralph	9	2	19	1	....	8	1	21	0
Insole	7	1	14	2	....	4	1	3	0
King						6	3	7	1

Umpires: P. Corrall and N. Oldfield.

heavens, Hampshire were all out for 116, and Trevor Bailey had taken 8 wickets in the innings for 49 runs from almost twenty-four overs. In all, he had taken 14 wickets and had scored 130 of his team's 271 runs in the game.

You might have found him in the poky Romford dressing-room just after that match, gear scattered everywhere, a quiet smile of contemplation on his face, a beer in one hand, a cigarette, the ash long, between the fingers of the other. He would not be prone to say much. What he did say would be of a technical nature. 'If we had brought in another slip earlier, we'd have had Jimmy before he made 20,' for instance. His curly dark head would be leaning back against the wall and he would, likely as not, in the words of Frank Tyson, 'be wearing a perfect expression, not of triumph, but of gentle self-satisfaction'.

An excellent May was translated into an excellent season. Besides Hampshire, Essex's match against the West Indians at Ilford earlier that month had provided Trevor with the opportunity to confirm his claim to being the foremost all-rounder in England, and he had used the opportunity to show that he was in a class of his own. Nine wickets in that match for just over 100 runs had been a fine start; and he built on it. It would be wrong to say that he was by now looking over his shoulder, but one or two shadows were just beginning to encroach on his own exclusive patch of sunlight. Brian Close's all-round abilities had not yet become a factor much beyond Yorkshire, but they were there for all to see. In addition, there was a young fellow at Cambridge whose batting had become the talk of the cricket world and who was reputed to be able to bowl more than bit. His name was Edward Dexter, known widely as 'Lord Ted', and he was seen as possible salvation for these who longed desperately for the preservation of the amateur influence in English cricket. There was, as yet, no comparison between him and Trevor in terms of all-round ability, but the spur was there, if one were needed.

7

The Last Tests

1958–59

Whatever the signs that the Test-match career of Trevor Bailey – now approaching thirty-five and presenting a comfortable though not portly figure to the world – was driving towards a close, they were not readily apparent during the summer of 1958. But it was not one of his best seasons. For the first time since 1948, he failed to score 1,000 runs in first-class cricket, although he took well over 100 wickets. The New Zealanders, poor souls, could make little of the English summer and provided scant opposition to the strong England team. There was a lack of incentive in the Test matches for Bailey, and nothing in the way of dramatic occasions to draw out of him that last ounce of effort which separated him from his fellows.

But he was generally there or thereabouts. He bowled economically in the four Tests in which he played, a mere sixty-six overs bringing him the handsome return of 7 for 93. His batting was scarcely required. England won the series easing up. They were the first team to win the first four Tests of a series in England, and Lock, Laker and Trueman proved too much for New Zealand on rain-affected wickets. In the first three Tests, the tourists made totals of 94 and 137 at Edgbaston, 47 and 74 at Lord's, and 67 and 129 at Headingley.

There was precious little here to provide an adequate testing-ground for the forthcoming visit to Australia. Even so, there were few quarrels with the team to tour Australia in 1958–59, selected somewhat oddly in late July, during the fourth Test at Leeds. It virtually picked itself, although some critics counted Dexter unlucky to have made a sparkling 52 in that match after the team had been selected. He made the trip down under eventually, though: he and John Mortimore of Gloucestershire were sent for to reinforce an injury-ridden and generally bedevilled England party under Peter May. Before the first Test match of the series even began, Willie Watson and Raman Subba Row had both sustained long-term injuries.

Bailey also developed during the tour an injury to his back which, in retrospect, he wishes he had not tried to shrug aside. Every time he put his front foot on the ground his back hurt and, although he was able to bat under this sort of discomfort, his bowling suffered badly. It was to be the last time he represented England, overseas or at home. He had lost some of his mobility, back problem or not, but under normal circumstances he was still the best bowling, batting, fielding all-rounder available to England. That this tour of 1958–59 should see the end of his Test-match career was the result of several factors, not the least of which was his slow scoring in Test matches, which for once failed to save the Englishmen's bacon. He was also being written off more and more as a monumental bore.

Greatly respected by team-mates and opposition alike for his tremendous fighting qualities, Trevor was nevertheless already an endangered species when the *SS Iberia* set sail for Australia under the management of Freddie Brown. Of the team Brown had taken as captain to Australia in 1950–51, Bailey and Evans were the sole surviving players. May's 1958–59 team was choc-full of good cricketers, and they were expected to retain the Ashes, but those injuries set them off on the wrong foot, and a number of other factors contributed to one of the worst records of any English team to visit Australia.

Whatever the prospects for Trevor's performance on this tour, the newish system of broken-time payments for amateurs had resulted in his obtaining a reasonable deal for himself. Even allowing for inflation, it was a great deal better than the £200 he had received as expenses for his first tour in 1950. A story about Jim Laker's conversation with Gubby Allen prior to that tour in 1958 illustrates the point. Laker recounted it in the following way: 'I told Gubby that I was considering becoming an amateur and I wondered how he would feel about this. He asked me if I'd given it serious consideration and said that, if I had, he thought it was absolutely splendid but wondered why I wanted to do this at that stage of my career. He didn't look best pleased when I told him that I thought I would be better off in financial terms playing as an amateur in the England team in Australia with expenses rather than drawing professional pay. I knew that this was true because Trevor Bailey told me he would receive £1,000, and I was due to get £800.'

Laker, of course, went as a pro – and a salty, well-seasoned old pro at that. Perhaps one of the chief failings of that 1958–59 team was that the 'old pro mentality' was too dominant, even among the younger players. Certainly, it was the least happy party Trevor accompanied down under. Speaking of that tour he says: 'On paper, we looked a powerful and balanced side with plenty of confidence and experience. We arrived expecting to return with the Ashes; instead, we were soundly thrashed. The sad feature was not so much that we lost, but that we failed to play to our potential and, even worse, surrendered without a reasonable fight.'

Trevor feels that part of the reason for this lay with the fact that the team tended to be too arrogant. Blasé and aloof, they were too ready to complain. The formation of cliques, even before things started to go wrong on the field, detracted from team spirit and saw groups of players drifting away from each other. The sinking of England without trace by a good, but unexceptional, Australian team, he puts down more to this than to the outbreak of throwing and dragging they encountered among the Australian bowlers.

In Bailey's view, the Australian 'chuckers' were just a convenient alibi, and an issue that had careered wildly out of control. It was a fact, of course, that the whole throwing question had gone too far without retribution, not only in Australia but throughout the world. It was also a fact that the England party contained two bowlers who were widely acknowledged in the county game to be suspect to the point of certainty. Peter Loader was thought to throw his bouncer and his wickedly-disguised slower ball, while Tony Lock, no-balled for throwing in the West Indies in 1952, was still carrying on without censure near the turn of the decade.

Umpires in England, poorly paid and beholden, had no wish to find themselves at the centre of a controversy off their own bat, and so certain bowlers continued to get away with it at home. Administrators throughout the world, to their discredit, failed to grasp the nettle. The English authorities, led by MCC, tended to lead world opinion, but they had done nothing about Lock or Loader. The MCC tour of Australia in 1958–59 was to prove the catalyst for an eruption, the dust from which was to take a long time to settle; and it tended to overshadow the enormity of England's failings in going down by four matches to nil in a Test series which left Australia with the Ashes for the first time since 1951. England's older stars were, it seemed, on the wane, Bailey, Evans, Watson and Tyson among them. The captaincy, too, suffered by comparison with that of Richie Benaud, lively and imaginative at the helm of the Australian effort. By comparison, May's leadership seemed to many to be stereotyped and uninspired. One way or another, cheer was not a commodity easily come by in the England camp.

The series also laid the seeds of the legislation, later introduced, to use the front foot rather than the rear one in determining a no-ball. For not only were there Australians who delivered the ball with a jerk, but some of them also 'dragged' well beyond the return crease before delivering the ball. Facing a fast 'chucker' was one thing; facing a 'dragger' who delivered from nineteen or twenty yards was another; facing a 'dragger' who also 'chucked' was a combination doubly to be feared. Then again, in some cases, these factors were made worse by the unusual angle of the ball when delivered by a left-arm fast bowler from over the wicket.

England's plan to counteract the left-arm over-the-wicket bowling of such as Davidson and Ian Meckiff, by employing left-handers early in the innings, was struck a double blow when Watson and Subba Row were injured early on. The normally reliable Peter Richardson suffered a terrible loss of form. For once, Trevor Bailey, called in to fill the breach as usual, was unable to make amends for these shortcomings. He was still pressed into service to open the batting in four of the five Test matches, to bear the brunt of the hostile, almost unknown Australian opening attack. But his efforts in the first Test did not meet with universal approval, even though he made top score for England in both innings, for Australia went on to win the game by 8 wickets.

The innings which brought all the opprobrium upon his head came after he had been switched from the No. 6 position he occupied in the first innings to No. 3, in order to shore up one end after an early loss, in the second. England had got away to an awful start in that first innings and had been dismissed, on a pitch not ideal for batting but by no means impossible, for 134 runs. Hence the decision to give Bailey the opportunity of blunting the attack second time round so that other, more free-scoring spirits could cash in.

The problem was that he accomplished his task all too well. His main task of blocking off one end was carried out effectively. The overall plan was set back initially, however, by the inability of others to fulfil to a more than minimal degree the part expected of them. By the end of the third day, in a match of uninterrupted play, each team had batted once, and England were 92 for 2 wickets in their second innings. Three full days had produced 412 runs. Bailey at that stage had made 27 runs in two hours and forty-five minutes out of England's second-innings total. Although the context of the match had justified his dogged defence, the general tempo of events had caused many people to wonder whether, in these conditions, Test-match cricket was worth playing at all.

The Australian over rate, like that of England, had been tardy. The inability of the England batting to cope with Meckiff, doubtful action and all; the need for England to build some sort of total, no matter how slowly; the great difficulty of increasing his run rate, once in a defensive groove: all these were factors uppermost in Bailey's mind when he and Tom Graveney took strike the following morning. Graveney's suicidal run-out weighed him down even more. But perhaps the crucial element in his determination not to relax his vigilance for one second was the dismissal of Colin Cowdrey, just as he was beginning to push the score along. For Cowdrey was given out, caught by Kline at leg slip, when, to most people watching, Kline had scooped up a ball which had bounced well in front of him. It was really up to Kline not to claim the catch but, if the thought crossed his mind, he kept quiet about it. Even a consultation between the umpires failed to produce the right answer.

Cowdrey was given out, and all Trevor's innate stubbornness was brought into play.

It was easy to write afterwards that his marathon innings which eventually lasted to within ten minutes of the close of the fourth day's play while he compiled 68 runs in seven hours and thirty-eight minutes, cost England as dearly as it proved frustrating to the Australians. If any innings were needed to brand Bailey in history as the 'Barnacle', the man who drove away the crowds who were fed up with the slow scoring, this was it. But it is now not difficult to see that, to some extent, he has been made a scapegoat for some desperately unenterprising cricket by both teams. The Test matches in Australia in 1958–59 were played over a six-day period, and the effect of this, at least psychologically, must have been to fulfil Parkinson's Law of work rates expanding to fill the time available. If Australia had not been threatened by a brewing storm, who knows how cagey they would have been while scoring the 147 runs needed for victory?

As it was, the threatening weather saw Norman O'Neill play the one lastingly aggressive innings of the match, Australia won by 8 wickets with a day to spare, and Bailey's effort was thrown into stark, somewhat unfair relief. Nobody else in the England team had come within sight of scoring a half-century in the match, but Bailey's innings has always been awarded more brickbats than praise. His 3 wickets for 35 runs in Australia's first innings had played their part in keeping England in the game. He had made another marked impact on the Australian scene without being given the credit he perhaps deserved.

There was no doubt, though, about the part he played in the New Year Test match at Melbourne. If he could be accused of misreading the position at Brisbane, there was no question of this happening here. Once more, he opened the innings. Once more, he was in danger of being marooned. This time, England lost their first three wickets for 7 runs, Bailey standing by helplessly as Richardson, Watson and Graveney all fell in the third over of the day, bowled by Alan Davidson. Whether stung by the critics or, more likely, spurred on by the needs of the moment, Bailey counter-attacked. He made 48 of the 85 runs added with May for the fourth wicket, before Meckiff, whose action was by now the subject of fierce public controversy, had him caught in the gully. He made the second highest score in England's second innings – 14, an innings exceeded by 3 runs by May, but by no other – as England were pushed aside by Meckiff's 6 wickets for 38 for a total of 87. This was England's lowest total in Australia since 1903 when, on the same ground, they had been dismissed for 61. It had been, with one or two honourable exceptions, Bailey among them, a dispirited and dispiriting display, and again it ended in defeat.

Trevor's back was by now painful when he bowled, and uncomfortable when he didn't; although he kept going until the end of the Australian leg of the tour, he did not go to New Zealand, consigning himself instead to a manipulative operation under anaesthetic. This enabled him to be fit for the 1959 English season, but came too late to affect the course of events in Australia.

Meanwhile, there were three more Test matches and a number of other difficult state games to surmount. It was a tour as notable for injuries to the MCC players as for much else that was unusual, and selection was often on the basis of who was fit enough to play. At Sydney, however, where the third Test was played, it was a considerable surprise when Dexter was picked ahead of Watson, but no surprise that Bailey should again be an automatic nomination to open the batting.

He batted with his usual phlegm but, along with the other faster bowlers, Trueman and Statham, bowled comparatively little. Laker and Lock were seen by May as the potential match-winners – a choice that was justified in that England came closer to winning than at any other time during the series. An injury to Meckiff early in their second innings meant that England were spared the need to face one of their principal tormentors for the remaining Test matches although, as it turned out, there were plenty more where he came from. Gordon Rorke, who replaced him for the last two Tests, was equally suspect of action, was also a dragger and, in nineteen years of Test cricket, was one of the fastest bowlers Trevor ever faced.

But it was his old adversary, Raymond Lindwall, who provided the last ironic twist of the knife at the end of this less than triumphant

137

venture for Bailey. It had been thought, with good reason, that Lindwall would be hanging up his boots soon after MCC's previous visit to the Antipodes in 1955. And it will be remembered that Bailey had presented his wicket to Lindwall in order that the great Australian fast bowler should be able to retire with the magical 100 wickets in Anglo-Australian Tests against his name. But here he was again, at Adelaide for the fourth Test, recalled to Australia's colours at the age of thirty-eight, and still a master of swerve and variation of pace. The arm was lower, the run-up less awesomely menacing, but Lindwall it was. The second England innings found Bailey defending stubbornly and well, having survived to bolster England for nearly an hour after they had followed on. Off the last ball of the day he played at Lindwall, the ball went to Wally Grout, the wicket-keeper, who took the ball down the leg side and appealed. Bailey was given out, though Lindwall himself had not uttered and Bailey had not hit the ball.

Worse was to come. In what was to be his final Test match, at Melbourne, Trevor bagged a 'pair'. This was bad enough. Even worse, though, was that in each innings he was out to Ray Lindwall. The great game of cricket has its gods, and they will not be mocked. You cannot play the game as hard as Trevor Bailey did, give your wicket away, even in the most generous manner, and expect to get away with it. By yorking Bailey all over the place in the first innings of the final Test of that 1958–59 series, without a run on the England score-board, Lindwall passed Clarrie Grimmett's record haul of 216 Test wickets. His joy, and that of the thousands of Australians watching at the time, was the sweeter because it was Bailey who had, this time most unwittingly and reluctantly, provided the wicket that achieved it.

For Trevor, philosophical as ever, it was all part of the game he had worked out better than most, but which experience told him could never be taken for granted. He was more concerned at his lack of contribution to the England effort than he was over the uninhibited joy of the Australian crowd, with whom he had enjoyed an unprecedented love-hate relationship, always tinged with fulsome respect, over the years. He was not to know for certain at that juncture – though the odds were heavily weighted against him – that this was to be the last time he was to hear the shouts of the 'ockers' as he came out to bat. Over three visits to their country he had given as good as he got, and they loved and hated him for it. Their cries of frustration as his forward defensive stroke kept Lindwall, Miller and the rest at bay, and England on an even keel, will live with him for ever, though he will not be so sentimental as to own to it. Always abusive, the barracking was sometimes touched by humour. 'Boiley, you're a statue. I wish I was a pigeon,' rung out one day at Melbourne. It was one of many such cries: they served only to inspire him to annoy them even more.

8

Elder Statesman

1958–67

At the end of that Australian tour, Bailey came home with the compensation of knowing that he had by no means disgraced himself in a team which had failed to live up to expectations. He knew he had not been at his best, but the next English season found him fit and determined. He was unlucky that the visitors in 1959 were those pleasant, gifted, but scarcely formidable cricketers from India.

Had an Australian team been visiting these shores, or one from South Africa or the West Indies, Bailey would surely have been picked to play for England again. As it was, his best ever domestic season was given no recognition whatever. He was not even selected once for England in a summer which saw him make 2,011 runs at an average of 46.76 and take exactly 100 wickets. The plain fact was that he was not needed. Almost any England XI could have won the series, and the selectors got away with murder – including fielding a Test team with Fred Trueman batting at No. 8 – and still won the series by five matches to none. There was no need, and therefore no place, for the Trevor Bailey brand of Test cricket.

Messrs Allen, Insole, Wooller and Sutcliffe, the selectors of the day, saw the opportunity to try out new blood without the risk of falling flat on their faces. The cry for brighter cricket had taken hold. In the case of Trevor, fame had turned to blame. His forthright and sometimes almost cynically defensive way of playing the game was to be sacrificed on the altar of a more Corinthian approach. England's poor results in Australia formed the perfect excuse to ditch the old guard, well as it had served.

The writing was on the wall when the first Test team was picked.

140

May, Cowdrey, Arthur Milton, Evans, Statham and Trueman were the only members of the eighteen-strong party who had gone to Australia to be selected for that first test at Nottingham in early June. By then, Trevor had scored nearly 500 runs for Essex, at an average of 70 – including two centuries and an undefeated 88 – and he had taken 22 wickets. In all, he scored six centuries that summer, more than any other all-rounder (Dexter by now was seen purely as a batsman), and only six other players scored more. Essex benefited from his presence to the extent that they won their first five Championship matches and were challenging strongly for the title at one time before having to settle for ninth place. They were a side greatly to be feared. But there could be no doubt that, in the minds of the England selectors, and therefore in terms of all practical possibilities, Bailey's day as an England Test player was done.

In the more relaxed atmosphere of a tour abroad, the sun on his back, the England selectors and others in authority off his back, as part of a team which looked towards him and up to him in times of difficulty, Trevor Bailey had been a superman. He had been on five tours: three to Australia (two of these including New Zealand), one each to the West Indies and South Africa. It is a measure of his worth that the only time during that period when he had failed to play in a Test match was in Australia in 1950–51, and then it took a broken thumb to keep him from being selected.

By the time the team to tour the West Indies in 1959–60 was announced, even Trevor had given up hope. Easy pickings against India, and the emergence of Ray Illingworth as a genuine all-rounder, were among the elements that spelt *finis* to a wonderful Test-match career. He had played a role in an era admirably suited to it. But he was type-cast by now, and the same plays were no longer being written. Public tastes had changed. Cricket was no longer the summer pursuit for spectators that it had been. They no longer flocked to see it. The dreaded 'magic box' had come into its own, and cricket needed to adapt itself to it, especially at the highest levels. Besides, the day of the amateur, even the 'shamateur', was almost done and a 'brave new world' was in the minds of some administrators, although it was to take a little time yet to dawn.

Still, Bailey's 2,000-run and 100-wicket double in 1959 earned him another page in the history books. It was the first time any Essex player had performed such a feat. It was also only the twentieth time that anyone had passed such a milestone. Nor, since then, has the achievement been equalled. Yet not this, but another record, which still stands against his name, is more likely to be associated with his career, to the detriment of his great natural all-round ability. It is the entry under *Wisden*'s 'Test Match Slowest Individual Batting Records'. T. E. Bailey,' it reads, 'England v Australia at Brisbane, 1958–59, 68 in 458 minutes.'

In some ways, it was just as well that there was no room for him in the team which embarked for West Indies under Peter May in December 1959. For England's time-wasting on that tour of the Caribbean became a matter of grave concern, and if he had been there he might have been blamed for it. England's early victory saw them doing everything to sit on the lead and, although they succeeded, an over rate of thirteen per hour could often be laid at their door.

Bailey had spent much of the 1959 season captaining Essex in the absence of Doug Insole. On duty as a selector or paying attention to business commitments, Insole was available less than usual, although he played often enough to make over 2,000 runs. The following year, his Test career over, Bailey stepped more and more into the breech. It was obvious that one of those natural breaks was about to occur: Insole to give up the captaincy, Bailey to step into his shoes or, more accurately, to continue to wear the shoes he had been trying on for some time. In this way, Bailey's life was stabilised into becoming the pillar of Essex cricket: secretary now in much more than name, captain in all but name. Busy otherwise with his various writing and promotional activities, found for him by Bagenal Harvey, he had now entered the end game in a cricketer's life. If he was sitting more comfortably than many who found themselves in a similar position, he deserved it. He had not gone out of his way to ingratiate himself at Lord's or anywhere else; he had performed nobly in his self-appointed tasks and he was still a man very near the top of his chosen career, and with a number of irons in the fire for the future.

Another successful season on the playing field accompanied his efforts in 1960, the last before he officially assumed the Essex captaincy. The county moved up to sixth place in the Championship, losing – as you might perhaps expect with Bailey often at the thelm – fewer matches than any other county. By modern standards, the sixth double of his career, with 1,639 runs at an average of nearly 40 and 117 wickets at just over 20 apiece, was a formidable record for someone unable to command a place in the England team as an all-rounder. Those who most often occupied the position for England that summer, Illingworth and Fred Titmus, came nowhere near it. Illingworth averaged something more than 25 with the bat and took fewer wickets; Titmus took the same number of wickets as Trevor but averaged only 27 with the bat. Peter Walker of Glamorgan filled the berth of all-rounder alongside Illingworth in the third Test match; Jim Parks of Sussex, who kept wicket throughout the series, could be described as yet another. But Walker's season produced 57 wickets at 29 apiece and a batting average of fewer than 17 runs per innings, although he was an excellent close-to-the-wicket fielder. The cynic might also have made a similar point about Jim Parks's wicket-keeping. England, it seems, were trying hard to fill the gap left by Bailey, with indifferent success.

As if to rub all this in – although it is doubtful whether the selectors even noticed – Bailey's performance against Yorkshire, that year's county champions, produced as good an all-round achievement as any, in that or any other season. Unlike the present, those were the days when defeating Yorkshire came the way of very few. Yet Essex went to Headingley in July and beat them for the first time since the war (*see* Appendix 2). In an atmosphere as near as you could get to a Test match, Bailey was supreme. He made 60 not out in the first Essex innings of 180, after going in when Essex had lost their first three wickets for 23 runs. He then took 7 wickets for 40 runs as Yorkshire were bowled out for 86. His 46 in the second Essex innings helped to see them to a total of 200 and a lead of 94; and, although Yorkshire did better at their second attempt, an analysis of 33–8–61–5 for Bailey not only clinched matters, but was appropriately achieved while England were playing

143

South Africa just across the Pennines in a match which saw a revival in South Africa's fortunes after a disastrous start to the series.

Although the job of secretary to a county cricket club must have been different in countless ways from that of today, when so many aspects other than cricket and the staging of home matches occupy the incumbent, the mind does boggle at the way Trevor had been able to guide the club, play for the county and play Test cricket, summer and winter, and undertake various promotional and business activities during the course of the year. Now, in 1961, as secretary and captain, he was able to devote himself entirely to Essex and to his wide-ranging personal interests; although in taking on the captaincy, he had merely replaced one string to his bow with another. In another sense, however, the whole tenor of his life was made simpler. He wielded great power within the club because, to all intents and purposes, he was the administration. As captain, he could assess his needs; as secretary, he could work towards achieving them; and, as a man widely respected and known throughout the country, the county and, indeed, the cricketing world, he was well placed to serve his employers.

Between the years of 1961 and 1966, the period of his captaincy, Bailey's strong suit was a capacity to see the potential in the young player of real ability. This hardly comes as a surprise – nobody would be better aware of the technical qualities required to succeed at the highest level – but it was something to which he gave much painstaking time as secretary and something which, as captain, he showed a rare skill in fostering. Barry Knight, a fine all-rounder, was already fairly well-establilshed in the Essex firmament when Bailey took over the reins, and was on the verge of the England team. The young Robin Hobbs was just beginning to make a mark as a leg-spinner, and Keith Fletcher was waiting in the wings as a sixteen-year-old.

From Frank Rist, the kindly and genial Essex coach and 2nd XI captain, would come these and other recommendations. The judgement required during those poor times for cricket, not least Essex cricket, was considerable. The pay for a young pro was negligible; the size of the staff was of necessity pared to the bone. Essex had been well served traditionally by an influx of amateurs from clubs around the county, and that had the added advantage of saving money; but times were now less kind to the young man who wanted to take time off from his regular job to play county cricket. Furthermore, the prospects for the game at the top level had become less than exciting. These were the days before the vast surge in income derived from sponsorship, properly organised one-day cricket, realistic fees from television, perimeter advertising and the like. And gates were dwindling. The limited resources at Essex CCC's disposal had become even more sparsely available, and the secretary's job was largely concerned with keeping the club's head above water, both financially and on the playing field.

Trevor says that he was fortunate in that he was blessed with a committee which took his advice on most things. A high proportion of them had played the game at a reasonable level, while those who had not were, unusually, inclined to leave the running of the club to those who knew something about it. His disappointments were few. He regretted then as now that, unlike Warwickshire and Worcestershire, Essex did not venture into the football pool business in the early 1950s. By the time they decided to do so, ten years later, they had missed the bus. Then there was the appeal to the county which failed because, he feels, there was no real focal point in a widely-disparate entity such as Essex, part-county, part-London, split into small factions and identifying less with the whole than with their own back yard. But towards the end of his time as secretary, Bailey played a large hand in a financial coup which was to give Essex the wherewithal to buy the freehold of the Chelmsford ground, by securing a generous interest-free loan from the Warwickshire Supporters' Association. This move, which created a focus for the county's activities, allied to the general influx of money into the game around this time, laid the foundation for the healthy, prosperous and successful club which was to make such an impressive mark on the face of English cricket in the 1980s.

On the field, in the early and mid-1960s, it was team spirit and, above all, a sense of humour that singled out Essex as a side. Trevor, a serious but, by now, always approachable figure, brought along some able young players but also contrived to maintain the fine blend of levity and efficiency which was the legacy of his predecessor, Doug Insole. His own form and that of the older stalwarts were still vital factors when he led Essex on to the field for the first time as official club captain on 29th April 1961.

The first Essex match that season was against Warwickshire at Edgbaston. It was no great surprise that, given the occasion, Bailey rose to it. An undefeated century and a haul of 4 wickets for 71 runs was a typical riposte to his new responsibilities. At thirty-seven, Trevor modestly came on as second-change bowler, but took the first 2 wickets, went on to bowl more economically than anyone, and made up in cunning for what he was just beginning to lack in speed and nip off the pitch.

It was a year of good results for Essex and for Bailey. He led the county to sixth place again in the Championship and achieved the double for the seventh time in his career, with 1,240 runs and 133 wickets. Six other players accomplished the feat in 1961, but Bailey took more wickets than any of them, and it must have been with a tinge – no more – of personal regret that he watched Benaud's Australians beat England by two matches to one. Particularly galling for him must have been England's second-innings performance in the crucial fourth Test at Leeds, when Benaud, bowling his leg-spinners round the wicket, found none of the English batsmen able to cope. England subsided from 150 for 1 to 201 all out when set 256 to win.

Trevor played in the 1961 Gentlemen v Players match at Lord's, as he did the following year in the last fixture of all, before the distinction between amateur and professional was abolished. One of the issues which had especially not endeared him to Lord's had been his apparent lack of enthusiasm for taking part in this fixture year in and year out. He had been, of course, by his blatant if excusable attitude towards money, one of the prime catalysts in the abolition of the amateur status. Perhaps because his whole approach to the playing of the game was so 'professional', he saw the Gents v Players matches at Lord's, in which he found himself up against former and present friends in the England XI, as something of a non-event, preferring the cut and thrust of a County Championship match. The other Gentlemen and Players games at Scarborough, in which he took part regularly, were fun, with no pretensions to being trials for greater things; they were part of a festival; important enough to play properly and, coming right at the end of the season, games which had a place in the scheme of things. This was especially so if you needed the odd few wickets or runs to complete the double.

Bailey sums up his attitude to the two events as follows. About Scarborough, he says:

'On one occasion, I won some bottles of champagne by going out to bat against F. S. [Trueman] wearing a yachting cap, and I once bowled an orange at Len Hutton. This trick had to be accomplished with a full toss, first ball after lunch. I managed that all right, and he was covered in the stuff. The crowd loved it, but there were some fairly terse comments from Len, including references to cleaning bills. You could only do that kind of thing infrequently, and sometimes it was overdone. The main thing was to ensure we got a finish as near to the last over of the match as possible, and it was remarkable how well some people managed to perform considering the way they had punished their system the night before.

'As soon as the day's cricket was over, we would repair to the pavilion bar to have drinks with all the players. Then it would be off to the Grand Hotel for a quick bath and change into black tie before descending to have drinks with the ladies, who were all in long dresses. It was all quite formal, and we were expected to circulate and be rather grand. I remember the consternation there was on the part of 'Shrimp' Leveson Gower when Billy Sutcliffe demanded that he had his pint of beer before we went in for dinner.'

Of the Lord's fixture, by the time he played in that last match in 1962, he says:

'The match did not mean as much as when I started in the

game. In my early days, it was a genuine Test trial. However, I
suppose my position was a bit special as the Gentlemen were
always short of bowling, and so I got picked a lot for them. I
enjoyed the matches, but they lacked the challenge of, say,
Essex v Yorkshire, when there was really something at stake.
One year, I declined an invitation to play for the Gentlemen.
I'd pulled a muscle in my back and I played instead for Essex
against Sussex. I did not bowl in the first innings but I batted
and had a turn with the ball in the second innings. I think I got
a few wickets. Anyway, I remember that Robin Marlar, who
would have been captaining Sussex in that match but who had
been chosen as my replacement for the Gentlemen, was livid. I
suppose this illustrated the way we approached the Gentlemen
and Players match, with less reverence than in my early days.'

In fact, Bailey got more than just a few wickets. Marlar's ire is
understandable. But whatever Bailey's feelings about the Gentlemen v
Players match at Lord's might have been in the middle of his career,
that last match of all in 1962 found him with a heightened sense of
occasion; a point or two to prove, maybe, in his fortieth year, and he
rose – as he always seemed to – to the special atmosphere. The event
took place on 18th, 19th and 20th July of that year (*see* Appendix 2).

The match was drawn. Bailey, batting at No. 9 of all places, had no
chance to contribute much with the bat. He was given first use of the
ball, though, and bowling from his favourite Nursery End he removed
Mickey Stewart and John Edrich of Surrey with very few on the board,
finishing with 6 wickets for 58 runs from more than thirty overs. When
the last man, Norman Gifford, was caught behind the wicket, the old
head went back in a familiar gesture as he took the proffered sweater
from umpire Rhodes. It was strangely apt that the last knell tolling for
the amateur in first-class cricket should have been accompanied by the
applause of Bailey's colleagues as they lined up to allow him to lead
them off the field at Lord's.

The year 1962 was another good one for Trevor; better than good, as
captaining Essex brought the best out of him. There was no time to get

bored, no place for it either. The double was achieved with comparative ease in one of his best all-round seasons. It was his eighth double and one of his most prolific in terms of both runs and wickets: nearly 1,500 runs at an average of more than 35 and 125 wickets at just over 20 apiece was a monumental effort for someone not averse to the odd cigarette or the odd drink, and whose training consisted of playing cricket, cricket and still more cricket. Barry Knight, his young protégé, also did the double that year and played for England against Pakistan, that year's tourists. Those were the days, too, when it meant something to play for your country against the tourists, and Trevor's Essex beat the Pakistanis by 9 wickets, thus becoming the first county to beat all touring teams to visit English shores. Trevor took 5 wickets for 47 runs in the Pakistanis' disastrous first innings of 133, a position from which there was no recovery.

It was a remarkable year. Various highlights in the field included a victory over Warwickshire after Essex had been behind on the first innings by 193; they made 414 for 5 in their second innings, and then bowled out Warwickshire so readily as to win by 86 runs. Bailey's contribution was 95 in the Essex second innings and 5 for 22 in Warwickshire's.

Then there was another coup. This was initiated off the field in a quiet chat between two old sweats, Trevor Bailey and Jim Laker. Jim described it thus: 'Trevor Bailey was the county secretary as well as the captain of Essex and, when we were coming back from playing in a charity match, he asked me whether I'd be willing to turn out for the county on the basis of amateur expenses. We were pretty relaxed about the whole thing, and although I didn't make any money I certainly wasn't out of pocket and I had a good time with my little swan-song. Indeed, I got really quite keen and, when we came to play Sussex, I remember that I did my damnedest when bowling against Ted Dexter. After an over or two, he got down to the non-striker's end and said, "You're trying a bit today, aren't you?" and I said, "Well, Skipper, I thought I might try and impress you sufficiently to ensure that I get chosen to play for the Gentlemen this year!" '

Laker played in only twelve matches, but picked up 51 wickets at an average of under 19 apiece, headed the county bowling lists and, perhaps less significantly, was awarded his county cap. In that match against Sussex which had Ted Dexter so worried, he took 6 for 49 in a 72-run victory. He so dominated the game against Kent at Dover as to take 13 wickets for 159 in the match. But he never was picked to play for the Gentlemen.

A young man who began to make his mark in that same season, while Laker and Bailey were enjoying their Indian – or rather Pakistani – summers, was a stripling of eighteen, Keith Fletcher. Although it was 1962 before he impressed the critics at first-class level, he was one whom Trevor had earmarked as an England player from the time he first saw him in the nets at the age of sixteen. The way things worked in those days is described by Trevor thus:

'Keith Fletcher came from a village school in Cambridgeshire. A conscientious careers officer visiting Keith's school was surprised to hear that Keith wanted to become a professional cricketer. It was the first time he had encountered this, and he took the trouble to inform Harry Crabtree, the sports education officer for Essex and also on the committee. Harry alerted me, and I arranged for Keith to play in an Essex Club and Ground match at the end of the summer and took part myself. I was impressed, not only by his obvious potential but also because he had what I term a cricket brain. Throughout the winter, Keith came to the Ilford indoor cricket school for nets. The way he was able to drive off the back foot on the up convinced me further that he would be challenging for a place in the 1st XI before he was eighteen. He was also one of the few players whom one could teach to hook without concern, because his initial reactions were so quick.'

It was considerably later in his spell as secretary/captain of Essex that Trevor went off to the West Indies on a Rothman's Cavaliers tour and brought off another satisfying stroke. This time he returned home from Barbados together with armfuls of cigars (cigarettes were by courtesy of Rothmans in those days), quantities of booze, and a piece of paper signed by Keith Boyce, a Barbadian all-rounder. Trevor had not heard of or seen Boyce before the trip but, on the strength of one match in which Boyce impressed with his lively bowling, powerful hitting and quite brilliant fielding – above all his throwing – he had signed him up before the close of play. Boyce was to become a great asset and drawing power on the Essex fields, although it was not until 1967, the year after Trevor had relinquished both the captaincy and the secretaryship, that Boyce qualified by residence and began to make his mark.

Bailey's playing days overlapped with the full emergence of Keith Fletcher by several years, however. Fletcher's first full season was 1963, and he reached 1,000 runs by the end of July. But the man who scored most runs and headed the batting averages that season was our old friend, the Boil, with 568 runs at an average of over 37. His bowling that year was useful but hardly lethal. 'Bailey Fails To Achieve Double' might well have been a headline at the end of that cricket season; for he took only 79 wickets for 29 apiece and played second fiddle to both Barry Knight and Jim Laker, although bowling more overs than anyone except Knight.

Whatever the reasons for that shortfall, he did better in 1964 by whittling down his bowling average: he took 70 wickets for under 24 apiece. But the days of the double were done, it seemed. And so it was to prove. The winding-down process had begun in that, his forty-first year, and there was no turning back, although he again headed the Essex batting lists in 1964, even if four players in the county side made more runs. This achievement owed something to his facility for remaining undefeated once he had established himself. With thirteen not-out innings to his credit, he outlasted everyone else in the team by a considerable margin. Indeed, on average, he contrived to remain undefeated in every second match he played that year.

But 1964 continued one undisputable highlight. It was the year in which Essex defeated the Australians, and it was fittingly accomplished at Southend, the scene of the famous 721 scored in a day by Bradman's men in 1948. Bailey's own part in terms of performance with bat and ball was modest, but his captaincy and the way he marshalled his

151

young flock earned high praise – and it was always, always had been, good to beat the Australians. For Trevor, captaining a winning side against them made the occasion doubly sweet; and it was marvellous, too, that it all happened within shouting distance of his own and his parents' home, where it had all begun.

That victory over the Australians was the first by Essex since 1905, and it was by the handsome margin of 6 wickets. Much was owed to Gordon Barker and Keith Fletcher, who both made centuries in Essex's highest score against any Australian team. The first day of the match virtually sealed the Australians' fate, and I was there to see Fletcher hit twenty fours in his 125. The *Sunday Telegraph* had sent me to Southend to do a piece for them, and I duly delivered a glowing account of the Essex performance. I was particularly enthusiastic about the young, gnome-like figure whose impeccable timing had so often left the fielders standing like statues. 'And when he was out,' I wrote, 'the crowd stood and applauded him all the way home.' New to the scribbler's trade as I was then, it was with a sense of shock that I read in the *Sunday Telegraph* the following morning: 'And when he was out, the crowd booed and applauded him all the way home.' There is nothing you can do or say after that, except hope that not too many people would notice.

Young Essex players were becoming noticed, though. Robin Hobbs, one of the last of the country's dying breed of leg-spinners, was chosen to accompany MCC to South Africa the following winter, and Barry Knight and Fletcher were among others of Trevor's young colts knocking loudly on the door, either then or within a short space of time. Meanwhile, the Essex captain/secretary/part-time coach/journalist/businessman/player was rapidly approaching a difficult decision. At the end of the 1964 season, he was approaching his forty-first birthday with a number of irons in the fire; a great love of cricket, especially Essex cricket, was still burning brightly inside him, but he knew that the world he had inhabited and enjoyed for nearly twenty years had been changing gradually and, more important, so had the elasticity of those muscles and tendons which had seen him through for so long. Then there was the future to consider. He surely had another year or two left of playing at first-class level; but what then? Stay with

Essex as secretary, perhaps? Go full-time into business with the chance of a bit of writing thrown in?

Looking back, Trevor believes he made a bad mistake at the end of 1964 in deciding to go on playing for another two seasons. But lack of adequate finances had forced Essex to reduce their staff to such an extent that they had virtually no reserve cover. Nor, as in the old days, was the odd amateur on tap to be called up at a moment's notice. This imposed a big strain on those who were there, not least on Trevor himself, and he had not taken to heart the necessity to train, and to forget, perhaps, some of his other money-making activities. As a player, he should have gone into semi-retirement, at least, at the end of 1964. But, if he was to continue as captain, that was obviously impossible. He decided to go on playing – and he was to pay for it. With the county's slim reserves, he was often inclined to play with injuries which would otherwise have been rested. In short, 1966, his last season as captain, was no less than disastrous for him and for his team.

Yet 1965 had seen Trevor pulling out all the stops. It was a remarkable effort. By his own admission, he had lost his ability to win matches. His pace was barely on the fast side of medium, his 'nip-backer' had become a 'bend-backer', more often finding the inside edge than the gap between bat and pad, as of old, or sending up a shout for leg-before which, with Brian Taylor behind the stumps, could be guaranteed to wake up any dozer on a hot summer's afternoon. Somehow, though, he was able to draw on what was left of those reserves that had served him so wonderfully well throughout his career, and 1965 saw him come within a whisker of his ninth double of 1,000 runs and 100 wickets: he was only three wickets short of the magical figure. If, as captain, he had bowled himself in the second innings of T. N. Pearce's XI against the South Africans at Scarborough in the last match of the season, it seems virtually certain that he would have reached the target. All players – even the South Africans – were notably generous on such occasions. Instead, the South Africans were bowled out twice in two days, suicide against the spinners being the chief cause rather than any high-pressure tactics from T. N. Pearce's captain.

For Essex, though, it was not a great year. They finished only two places above Nottinghamshire at the foot of the table, and uncertainty as to the future captaincy of the club and the secretaryship was already beginning to brew. But, instead of leaving it at that and turning all his energies to being secretary, Bailey, suffering perhaps from a touch of hubris in the wake of a fine season, decided on just one more. The results were not good.

According to the club records, the 1966 season was preceded by a certain amount of jockeying for position between the committee and Trevor. The official history of the Essex County Cricket Club puts it this way:

'Towards the end of the 1965 season, it was felt that it was essential for the club to have a full-time secretary, and that it was placing too much of a burden on Trevor Bailey's shoulders for him to undertake the joint tasks of captain and secretary. Bailey was therefore offered the position of full-time secretary at an increased salary. After consideration, he decided not to accept the offer, feeling that he could be of considerable use as a playing member during the next season, which would be a vital one for the club. He did not wish to leave the playing scene with the county languishing in their present unhappy position. Trevor Bailey was thanked for his understanding and co-operation, and it was decided to advertise for a full-time secretary. As a result, Major C. A. Brown was appointed to this post, to commence his duties on 1 January 1966.'

This left Bailey with the captaincy and, if there was any doubt as to whether this would be his final season, his own mind was made up quickly when he badly tore a muscle in his right thigh in a fixture with Derbyshire during the recently-initiated Gillette Cup and then perforce went on playing. This left him with a large hole in his right thigh which is there even to this day and which had a debilitating effect on his performances throughout the rest of that last unhappy season.

It was a year that began ominously. The first County Championship match was at Leicester. First, rain prevented play on either of the first two days. Then, on the third day, when some play was possible, T. E. Bailey retired in mid-innings with a thigh strain, his season only a couple of hours old. A week off for Essex came fortuitously, and Trevor was on parade again for the next match against Warwickshire at Edgbaston, where he himself made little impact on the score-book, although his team lost a nerve-tingler by only 24 runs. The Ilford week, when Essex played Somerset and Gloucestershire, saw him strike form with the ball. Four wickets for 37 runs from twenty-one overs in Somerset's first innings, and two economical spells against Gloucestershire in drawn matches kept his head above water – and there was plenty of it about that year. But then came the Gillette Cup match against Derbyshire.

It has often been said that Bailey would have been a one-day player *par excellence*, with his controlled bowling and his ability to size up situations ahead of most others. Certainly, his performance against Derbyshire, in a game which saw him bowl ten tight overs and make 38 runs before being run out, did nothing but reinforce that opinion. Essex won the match by 2 wickets, just as Trevor intended, but the further damage he did to his thigh was both unwelcome and unexpected; and it contributed to a gravely disappointing last campaign for him. He was forced to rest for two weeks, but that was not long enough. The rest of the season was a battle against his handicap, one long struggle for runs and wickets. He managed to play in twenty of Essex's twenty-eight County Championship matches, but he struck with his bowling less often than before. His batting, also, was hampered. A top score of 31 not out from thirty-three innings was an indication of the way things went.

Not much consolation was to be had from the overall performance of his team. From fifteenth place in the championship in 1965, they moved to sixteenth in 1966. Even his ambition to lead Essex away from the bottom of the table had come to nought. But even if the wickets were not falling as they used to, it was fitting that his last bowling stint of that season should bring him the nice little analysis of 9–4–14–2. It was in a match against Somerset at Taunton which the home team won by 101 runs – no disgrace in that, for Somerset won a lot of matches that season, and Essex went down with all guns blazing. But Trevor had wanted much more, for himself and for his team.

There were other reasons why Trevor felt that the end of his tenure might have been happier. He had lobbied hard for Barry Knight to succeed him as captain in 1967. An all-rounder of outstanding talent, cast in a similar mould to Trevor himself, but lacking Bailey's extraordinary powers of concentration, Knight was known to be unhappy about the possibility of serving under the only other likely candidate. But the committee came down finally on the side of the sergeant-major-like qualities of their wholehearted wicket-keeper, Brian Taylor, and Knight upped sticks and went to Leicestershire which, at the time, Trevor considered to be something of a disaster. In fact, Taylor proved in many ways to be just the captain Essex required and later brought from Bailey the not inconsiderable praise of having done 'an extremely able job in his own distinctive way.'

A few games for Essex under Taylor followed in 1967, but by now the need to secure the future was taking up a large part of Trevor's waking moments.

Epilogue

In purely cricketing terms Trevor's decision in 1964 to continue playing was wrong. And there are occasions, too, when he looks back and wonders whether accepting Essex's offer of the full-time secretaryship might not have been the best course for him to have taken. At the time, though, his decision was probably as clear-cut as these things ever are. There was little sign of much money coming into the county game. Various ways of pulling free of the depression which surrounded the first-class game were under active consideration; but the Clark Report – the product of a distinguished committee which, under the chairmanship of David Clark, had sat for a long time – which advocated more one-day cricket had received scant support from the county clubs. Sponsorship on any scale had neither been contemplated seriously enough nor sought with vigour.

On the face of it, greater opportunities lay outside the game's official organisation, tempting though it must have been for sentimental reasons to remain in the bosom of the family. Trevor's agent, Bagenal Harvey, had forged close links with Rothmans, the tobacco giants, and there was promotional work to be had there. Then there were Trevor's links with the journalistic world. His powers of observation and shrewd tactical insight were a considerable asset in that field of activity, his very name another; and if his prose was unlikely to cause the likes of Neville Cardus or Geoffrey Green any loss of sleep, he wrote fearlessly in a straightforward, if understated, style.

He also had some money. A testimonial, awarded in his last year with Essex, had raised less than might have been hoped, but for some time there had been all those bits and pieces to go alongside what Essex had paid him. So the possibility of investing that money in business in his native county, where the commercial opportunities of the new town

157

Basildon beckoned, was also a strong incentive to try his luck in the outside world, in areas where his cricketing fame could be used to advantage.

Trevor had never been obsessed with the idea of making a fortune. Cricket had given him a good life. He had seen the world in the most comfortable of circumstances, had managed to give a public school education to his children, had a nice house, fame and a number of friends and acquaintances throughout the world, had his head firmly screwed on to his shoulders. All he wanted now were alternative ways of producing a life, *sans* the playing of serious cricket, similar to that to which he had long been accustomed.

Some of the routes by which he accomplished this have been mentioned. His chief immediate lifelines after leaving the employ of Essex were the *Financial Times* and the *Observer*, Rothmans, and the BBC. Meanwhile, Bagenal Harvey's stable of thoroughbreds – a string which included Denis Compton (from way back), Tom Graveney, Colin Cowdrey, Frank Tyson, Garfield Sobers, John Arlott and, from other spheres, Jimmy Greaves, Jimmy Hill, David Coleman, George Eastham and Polly Elwes, wife of Peter Dimmock, head of BBC sport – were pleased to have the name of Trevor Bailey in their midst. And from this particular source, from after-dinner speaking to cricket promotion throughout the world, jobs were to be had, the rewards for which were far from meagre.

Just as he had been prepared to move up and down the England batting list, from opener to No.6 and back again, Trevor was a willing horse when it came to serving his new masters. He could be relied on to do what was necessary. From the start of his new life he found a happily complementary mainstream existence: writing for the *Financial Times* and commentating on *Test Match Special*, one of the longest-running cult soap operas connected with any game. He had begun writing for the *Financial Times* while still playing for Essex in the early 1960s. Now he became their cricket and association football correspondent. This involved writing a piece for every Monday edition, winter and summer, as well as covering the day-to-day progress of Test matches in summer and any midweek soccer internationals in the winter months. It was in many ways a plum job. Though insufficient of itself, or in combination with *Test Match Special*, to keep the home fires burning as custom demanded, both activities nevertheless fitted in well with his more lucrative promotional work.

And there was glamour: the work took him all over Europe during the football season, and it had the advantage of keeping him in touch with both of the games he had played with such skill. The wear and tear associated with the journalist's life he took in his stride. He knew his way around and, as newspapers go, the *Financial Times* was less demanding than most. The average reader was not that interested in quotes from participants in the various games, or from beleaguered football managers. It remained one of the few papers which still believed that the correspondent covering an event is more likely to have a credible, unbiased view of what goes on than someone who, by the nature of his involvement, is bound to be one-eyed. The average reader of the *Financial Times* wanted to read what had happened, written by someone whose opinions he respected. The less garnished the style, the better.

Trevor fulfilled this role well. He could be as technical as he liked, and he was pleased by that. He could virtually pick his own assignments, and that suited him. Furthermore, he was a big fish in the comparatively small pond occupied by sport in that unique pink newspaper, and he could swim about unhampered by predatory rivals.

Holding his own with *Test Match Special* was a different proposition, but he has coped quite admirably with that over a period of some twenty-five years, largely by virtue of his own individual self-contained approach and a way of delivering pronouncements which make you feel that he knows what he is talking about. You feel, too, that if the players out in the middle only knew what he was saying they might well be revising their tactics to agree with him. Nasal, though not noisy, his voice and manner have been perhaps better suited to the task of summarising in expert fashion rather than to ball-by-ball commentary. Both his expert knowledge of the game and his terse style of delivery testify to that. Not the 'Voice of Cricket' – that will always be John Arlott's – but certainly the cricketer's man on the spot. Not always right, but always prepared to give a view, and unmistakably perceptive: that has been Trevor's niche.

Trevor is the longest-serving member of the *Test Match Special* team, senior in that respect even to Brian Johnston. He made his first broadcast in 1966 and has continued, virtually uninterrupted, ever since. It was therefore appropriate that Arlott's last words as a Test-match commentator should have included the phrase: 'And now, after a few words from Trevor Bailey, it will be Christopher Martin-Jenkins.'

Talk to his friends and colleagues on the programme, or to his producer, Peter Baxter, and you find precious little difference of opinion about his qualities or his foibles. They are at one when it comes to describing his delivery as the modern version of Dickens's Mr Jingle in *Pickwick Papers*. Clipped phrasing very much to the point, an economy of words, no mincing about are his hallmarks. Baxter feels he missed a chance of the ultimate 'Mr Jingle' phrase when, at the Oval in 1979, Dilip Vengsarkar, the Indian batsman, edged a ball from Bob Willis to David Bairstow behind the stumps. Bairstow missed the catch, the ball going through his gloves on to the boot of Michael Brearley, standing at first slip, and thence to Ian Botham at second slip, where it was caught. 'Good ball – bad shot – poor wicket-keeping – nice kick – fine catch,' would have been his staccato reaction to this chain of events.

Johnston has pointed to Bailey's sense of humour (both share a fondness for excruciating puns) and describes his broadcasting as safe, unhurried, reliable and, at times, provocative. Both he and Baxter are quick to point to his willingness to stick out his neck in forecasting the pattern of play, his critical awareness of what constitutes poor cricket, and the alacrity with which he deplores it – although he often leaves it to his sardonic sense of humour rather than any downright condemnation to convey it. The modern cricketer is inclined to shrug aside comments made by former players. It is, they say, a different game these days. And, anyhow, who is Trevor Bailey? What did he do? What does he know about it? Trevor is proved right often enough to belie that all too frequent attitude. After all, the basics of cricket do not change. If a nightwatchman tries to hit a six, it is bad cricket; a late call for a run is bad cricket; and so is it bad cricket when a medium-paced bowler fails to bowl the right line and length to a particular batsman, or to bowl to his field or, indeed, to set the right sort of field. These are a few of Trevor's *bêtes noires*, just as they were when he was playing.

If his reactions are different from the typical Fred Trueman explosion of 'I don't know what's going off out there!' they are the more devastating for that. In fact, he is the perfect foil to Fred, just as he was on the field. An occasional lapse from the purities of the English language laces his speech. The word 'literally' has been noted as one of his failings – as in 'Tavaré has literally dropped anchor', or 'Willis has literally got his tail up'.

Trevor has found that the most difficult part of being a summariser, rather than a commentator, is the danger of sometimes opposing the commentator. For commentators are employed chiefly for their gift of the gab, their rounded vocabularies, their voices, at the same time sympathetic to the ear and informative. The summariser is by nature the expert, the chap who has played the game at the highest level and knows at least as much by experience as the players out there in the middle. The difficulty sometimes arises of a conflict of opinion as to what actually happened. If the summariser knows, for instance, that the googly so graphically described by the commentator is not in the bowler's armoury and that it was, in fact, a straight ball that achieved the wicket, should he be honest and say so? Or if a nick through the slips has been described as a late cut, what then? The answer for Trevor usually has been to allow the commentator absolute credibility, unless it is an error which would look foolish in the paper the following morning. Of course, there have been times when even Trevor has been wrong. Baxter says that he has always been impressed by the fulsomeness of his admission when such an event has occurred – and that is entirely in character. A sharp-eyed observer and stern critic, he has throughout his life never failed to be his own sternest critic.

Trevor's admiration for Arlott shines through when he is prevailed upon to talk about his colleagues. He envied John his gifts and his facility with words. 'Now here is van der Bijl coming in to bowl, looking like a younger, taller version of Lord Longford . . . (pause) . . . but not nearly so tolerant,' is one of Trevor's favourites. Indeed, it does go well with Arlott's gem, before the days of *Test Match Special*, when he described the bowling of South Africa's Tufty Mann when he was tying England's George Mann in all kinds of knots as 'Mann's inhumanity to Mann'. The van der Bijl remark might, though, have owed something to Alan Ross's classic about the portly Fred Rumsey 'bearing an unnerving resemblance to Sir Christopher Soames'. And it was Ross, too, who in at least one edition of the *Observer*, before it was spotted, described the bowling action of New Zealand's Bob Cunis, a medium-fast bowler who bowled off the wrong foot, as being 'like his name, neither one thing nor the other'. But that is to digress too far from *Test Match Special*, which is a programme of and for less sophisticated minds.

Bailey's view of his colleagues throughout his twenty-five-year stint is both kindly and occasionally waspish, as in: 'The *Test Match Special* team I joined in 1966 contained two summarisers, Freddie Brown and Norman Yardley; three principal commentators, John Arlott, Alan Gibson, Brian Johnston; an overseas representative; Bill Frindall as scorer; Jim Swanton, who delivered a daily close-of-play sermon; and Michael Tuke Hastings, who produced the programme from his headquarters at Broadcasting House.' But that was before the programme developed into something which Greta Bailey has been known to call a *Goon Show* with a cricketing theme. There is a light- heartedness about *Test Match Special* which Trevor's sense of humour well fits into as one of the straight men – it is all too easy to be too serious about cricket, a fact he recognises – but there is an audience out there that needs to know what is going on when it is going on. And the danger is that sometimes they have to wait until the latest cake from a well- wisher is described. It remains an intensely popular radio show, however, the recipient of mail from all over the world and a positive triumph for the will of the people over the minds of some BBC moguls, who several times have tried to cut down its air time, only to be frustrated by popular demand.

The broadcasting life has taken Bailey to South Africa, Australia and India. Radio has kept his name before the cricketing public of the world, and it has combined well with his other activities such as journalism, after-dinner speaking, and the conducting of parties to some foreign clime, where he and Greta play host once a year to whomsoever has the wherewithal to follow cricket and the England team. Off they will go to those often exotic and lovely places where the sun shines, while those in England groan under the burden of winter. He has always, it seems, had life worked out pretty well.

There have been other, more trying periods, though. His *alter ego* as a public-relations-cum-promotions consultant opened his eyes in the early days to the vicissitudes of the world of big business and to the extraordinary inefficiency of some of the people in that world. The obsession of many of them with keeping their noses clean, at the expense of doing a good job, was all at odds with his own happy view of life and the straightforward approach. Happily, this was never the case with one of his earlier clients, Rothmans, who had invested fairly heavily in cricket both in England and other countries, including their birthplace, South Africa. Together with others in the Bagenal Harvey stable, it was an early task of Bailey's to ensure the smooth running of the Rothmans Cavaliers, soon after he had finished playing for Essex. There were few problems here; indeed it was an ideal situation. Bagenal Harvey Associates organised both the sponsorship, through Rothmans, and television coverage with BBC2 and, using players under contract to county clubs, they staged a series of Sunday cricket matches throughout the summer on a forty-overs-a-side basis. The Cavaliers teams consisted in the main of recently retired and current top-class cricketers, and they would be pitted against the local county beneficiary's team or some such. Since the counties themselves were playing no worthwhile one-day cricket on Sundays, the matches were extremely popular with spectators and television viewers alike. Rothmans achieved excellent publicity. The cricketers taking part were reasonably rewarded. BBC TV was in the happy position of broadcasting cheapish television with good ratings, and various beneficiaries up and down the land were delighted with whatever came their way. And it was a useful source of income for Bagenal Harvey and his boys.

There is always a snag, however. The counties themselves were on their uppers, they were providing the players for this bonanza and were paying them, and they were getting virtually nothing in return. So it was that the John Player League was born; but only after a battle royal between those of us who were working for MCC at the time on the one hand and the Bagenal Harvey organisation, certain elements in television, and a whole host of figures in the game on the other. It was the first and only time I have found myself on the opposite side to

Trevor. He felt, possibly rightly, that MCC were too confrontational. But it was no fun being ranged against a powerful and influential organisation like Bagenal's. They tried every trick in the book to prevent the Sunday League getting off the ground, and convinced the Michael Parkinsons of this world and others that the cricket authorities were both misguided and doomed to failure. But we were determined that, if the counties' own competition on Sundays was to succeed, television was essential; and it simply was not possible to avoid competing with the Cavaliers, rather than co-existing with them, while they used our players for their own ends. And from 1968 onwards, instant cricket though it may be, the Sunday League has proved its worth in many ways, financial and otherwise. One of the first of our detractors to acknowledge this, in the most wholehearted way, was Trevor.

His adaptability and mastery of the art of practical expediency was severely tested in other ventures, though. A spell of working side by side with Ford in a cricket promotion left him with few illusions about the ways of the multi-nationals in the early 1970s. He had grown used, as he says, to the double-speak: 'Positive thinking', 'optimum client visibility', 'high and low profiles', 'learning curves', 'quality creative expertise', and the like. He had realised, too, the prime maxim of never saying on one sheet of A4 what you can say on twenty. What he had not realised, until his spell of working for Ford, was the way in which the buck could be passed as readily as a hot potato from one executive to another if there was any chance of expenditure being laid at a particular door.

Those were the days when Ford were setting off on a number of dubious schemes. Sponsoring Joe Bugner was, on the face of it, a good idea. What had not been appreciated was that, although considerable publicity was garnered from having Ford's name writ large on the boxer's silk dressing-gown before a televised heavyweight fight, less honour and glory were forthcoming when a badly beaten boxer, with the same silk dressing-gown draped round his shoulders, and the same name clearly visible, was helped, groggy and forlorn, from the ring. It was not, in the jargon, very good for 'product image'.

The cricket scheme, with which I had something to do on cricket's side of the fence, was not a bad one. A sum of money and a car for each county, with attendant publicity for Ford, was a good proposition for the game in those days of penury. But, for poor old Trevor, it was apparently a case of chasing from pillar to post and accomplishing little because of a lack of support from within the company. It all culminated in his being left with only ten days in which to organise a reception and send out invitations to the press and players and cricket administrators. But, since no account had been taken of the fact that the chosen date happened to coincide with the opening of the Motor Show, a late change to even that late decision left Trevor, for the first time in his life probably, in near hysterics. A lot of people, especially in Australia, would have paid a lot of money to see that.

He was better blessed by other ventures. Since its opening in 1955, he had been associated, financially as well as administratively and as jack-of-all-trades, with the Ilford indoor cricket school. His many other activities since then have enabled him to spend only a limited time on the school for which, he says, he was not the driving force, more of a figure-head, though not entirely a decoration. He gives much of the credit for the success of the venture to Harold Faragher, an Essex player and former captain of Ilford CC; the early years saw him spending his winter evenings coaching there before lifting the nets and preparing the venue for indoor bowls the following morning. Trevor believes that this example of entrepreneurial enterprise, while not making a great deal of money, has been a considerable asset to Essex CCC, whose players have received free practice facilities and used the place for pre-season training, again without payment. Now, of course, there is a new indoor school at Chelmsford, run by the county club itself. But Ilford continues to do all right.

Another achievement which he rates as a major accomplishment concerns the now thriving Wrigley Soft Ball Cricket Tournament for the very young. A chance remark from Gary Sobers, who believed that the soft ball approach, used in Barbados for reasons of economy, would be of real value to young people in Britain where, for all the coaching available at some levels, many small boys with an eye for a ball were rarely given the chance to play any form of cricket. From enlisting the support of the National Cricket Association in the shape of Brian

Aspital and Keith Andrew (who had toured Australia with Trevor and knew a good idea when he saw one), and also the backing and help of the English Schools Cricket Association, Trevor saw the project through. He obtained commercial sponsorship from the excellent Wrigley company, which jumped at the chance to be linked with a soft ball tournament for primary schools. Begun in the 1980s, it is still going strong.

Soft ball cricket is not to be confused with the American softball, a form of baseball. It is rather, and quite distinctively, a form of cricket, played with a soft ball and with a simple set of rules. It has the great advantage of bringing those playing it into the game for long passages of time, and it can be played almost anywhere. Fast-moving and involving all children taking part, not only those especially gifted, it is a game that can be played within a recreational period of no more than an hour. It is perhaps an organised form of most people's first experiences of cricket in London on concrete, or at the seaside on sand, from the times when two teams were first formed from a gang of boys anxious to hit a ball with a bat. It is fun to play, and it rewards the batsman who obeys the cardinal rules of getting into line and playing with a straight bat. Trevor is convinced of its merits. Anything that is fun and gets the vast majority of those neglected masses playing the game, and becoming used to hitting a ball with a bat, must be good for cricket at large.

Looking back, Trevor is inclined to think that he was not the world's best businessman. A couple of sports shops which he managed in the Essex area were not a great success, nor was he any more fortunate as manager of a toy wholesale business. On the sports goods side, he quite enjoyed – unsurprisingly – being busy selling to a continual stream of customers. 'Unfortunately,' he says, 'this seldom occurred, except over the Christmas period; but there are few more satisfactory sounds than ringing up sales on a till in the knowledge that some of that money – though never in the quantity I would have liked – is coming your way.' Now there is a statement that has the absolute ring of truth.

As for the toys, he much enjoyed the trade fairs at places like Harrogate and Brighton, was fascinated by the problem of second-guessing the tastes of the public, and survived an hilarious week or two in Hong Kong, where he was optimistically buying toys for his company. His problems centred round the purchase of a range of cheap toy cars. He intended to drive a hard bargain and was insistent that four particular models were just what he wanted but, at two shillings and eleven pence each, were too pricey by half. His negotiations were conducted through an interpreter. At the end of a long and difficult session he was assured that, after one or two minor adjustments, his price would be met. Samples were made, packaged and prepared for his inspection. It was not until he opened his parcels in the seclusion of his hotel room that he realised that the 'minor adjustments' meant the chrome being stripped off and the windows removed, so that the toys did not resemble cars at all. It was then a matter of picking himself up, dusting himself off and starting all over again. But he was good at that, and in the end his forward defensive proved too much even for the Chinese.

Now in his seventieth year, Trevor is still on the look-out for a good wheeze. He commentates. He talks at dinners. He writes for news-papers, mainly for the *Daily Telegraph* and *The Cricketer*. He still conducts touring parties all over the world to watch England play. There is little he will not do to earn an honest buck, renew old friendships, spend a week or two in the sun with the lovely Greta and a few cricket enthusiasts. A meticulous planner, he still fits a very full life into every twenty-four hours. He also works hard on behalf of the Lord's Taverners when he has a minute or two to spare.

When I wanted to meet him at one stage to discuss various aspects of this book, I was given an insight into the way it all goes. No answer from his house over a period of a couple of weeks meant that he was away. When I finally got hold of him, it transpired that he had been speaking at a couple of cricket dinners. At one, he stood in for Denis Compton who, through illness, was unable to fulfill an engagement. The other had been arranged long since. One of them, well, that was in Barbados; the other, believe it or not, was in Johannesburg.

That sort of pattern, so much a part of his career in cricket, has remained intact throughout the rest of his life. Like Barkis, Trevor is willing. If he believes an idea has some merit, he will try to put it into practice and he will succeed more often than not. Just as the young boy at school was prepared to take up bowling leg-breaks, the mature cricketer was prepared, at the request of Len Hutton, to open the batting for England. And when England wanted an accurate, third seam-up bowler, and not a striving quickie with a double arm whirl in his action, so he adapted.

It says everything for his skills as a cricketer, and for his character, that he was able to do that. Len Hutton's words about him, quoted on page 87 of this book, have a clear ring of truth. Throughout the whole of his career in cricket, Bailey's rare talents enabled him to adapt to the demands made of him when a gap occured in England's ranks and gave his presence a quality of indispensability. Throughout the 1950s and beyond, the thought of going on tour without Trevor Bailey was never entertained. The purse of MCC and the counties was not full enough to consider jetting out replacements at the drop of a hat; and with Trevor in the party there was seldom the need, so great was his versatility.

One of the more frequent criticisms levelled against him has been his inability to break free of the cocoon of concentration which led to his great defensive innings; to break the defensive mould, so to speak. This was certainly true at times, especially in his later years as a cricketer, although it has been much exaggerated. The fact is, though, that he was picked for his defensive qualities, above all others. He was keenly aware of his responsabilities to his team and sometimes saw them differently from others. On occasion he was wrong; more often than not, he was proved right in his judgement of what was necessary.

So it is now. He is happy and settled, a doting grandfather, living in his beloved Westcliff-on-Sea. He still takes a keen interest in local club cricket; he is prepared, always, to take on yet another task connected with the game. At a recent dinner to celebrate the association of Benson and Hedges with the game of cricket over a period of twenty-one years, Trevor was there as one of the longest serving, most regularly attending, always reliable men who throughout had been presenter of the B and H Gold Award to the man-of-the-match at games up and down the country. He has not been known to miss a dinner given annually at Lord's for past and present county secretaries. The game has been his life and it is still a large part of it. And he has taken care of himself and is content.

Appendix 1

Batting and Bowling Statistics

As a batsman: in all first-class matches in England

Year	Mats	Inns	Not out	Runs	HS	Av	100s	50s
1945	1	1	0	20	20	20.00	0	0
1946	11	16	3	412	97*	31.69	0	2
1947	26	43	9	1,277	205	37.55	3	6
1948	24	34	8	700	66*	26.92	0	3
1949	30	50	11	1,380	93	35.38	0	10
1950	27	42	4	1,041	82*	27.39	0	9
1951	31	44	8	1,096	104*	30.44	1	5
1952	36	56	15	1,513	155*	36.90	1	5
1953	28	42	9	1,278	84	38.72	0	10
1954	29	47	6	1,344	108*	32.78	1	8
1955	28	50	12	1,429	152*	37.60	3	5
1956	25	38	11	1,186	141*	43.92	3	4
1957	27	42	8	1,322	132	38.88	2	9
1958	29	44	4	904	90	22.60	0	5
1959	33	55	12	2,011	146	46.76	6	10
1960	32	48	6	1,639	118	39.02	1	11
1961	33	54	9	1,240	117*	27.55	1	4
1962	31	53	12	1,460	124*	35.60	1	9
1963	33	54	12	1,568	122	37.33	1	10
1964	31	46	13	1,106	89	33.51	0	6
1965	32	51	11	1,026	91	25.65	0	5
1966	23	37	9	627	77	22.39	0	1
1967	11	21	3	359	64	19.94	0	1
Total	611	968	195	25,938	–	33.55	24	138

* not out

As a bowler: in all first-class matches in England

Year	Overs	Mdns	Runs	Wkts	Av	Catches
1945	27.3	4	103	2	51.50	0
1946	284.2	58	903	37	24.40	14
1947	727.4	132	2,178	82	25.56	13
1948	646.4	130	1,984	63	31.49	16
1949	1,020	186	3,146	130	24.20	14
1950	736.1	187	1,842	88	20.93	18
1951	875.1	245	1,941	91	21.32	20
1952	1,171.1	278	2,997	103	29.09	20
1953	876	197	2,285	86	26.56	18
1954	864.1	200	2,161	101	21.39	16
1955	835.3	198	2,129	89	23.92	12
1956	672.3	176	1,697	78	21.75	22
1957	738.3	207	1,771	104	17.02	24
1958	876	236	1,918	113	16.97	24
1959	880.5	176	2,469	100	24.69	34
1960	1,047.1	279	2,370	117	20.25	23
1961	1,187	281	2,795	133	21.01	22
1962	1,092	297	2,574	125	20.59	15
1963	936.5	218	2,301	79	29.12	9
1964	791.5	219	1,665	70	23.78	13
1965	933.3	290	1,917	97	19.76	25
1966	440	106	1,028	45	22.84	15
1967	181.4	49	382	12	31.83	4
Total	17,842.1	4,349	44,556	1,945	22.90	391

As a batsman: in Test matches in England season by season

Year	Opps	Mats	Inns	Not out	Runs	HS	Av	100s	50s
1949	N Zealand	4	5	2	219	93	73.00	0	2
1950	W Indies	2	4	1	145	82	48.33	0	1
1951	S Africa	2	3	0	109	95	36.33	0	1
1952	India	—	—	—	—	—	—	—	—
1953	Australia	5	7	0	222	71	31.71	0	2
1954	Pakistan	3	3	1	81	42	40.50	0	0
1955	S Africa	5	9	1	184	49	23.00	0	0
1956	Australia	4	5	1	117	33	29.25	0	0
1957	W Indies	4	4	1	5	3	1.66	0	0
1958	N Zealand	4	4	1	39	17	13.00	0	0
Total		33	44	8	1,121	—	31.13	0	6

As a bowler: in Test matches in England season by season

Year	Opps	Mats	Overs	Mdns	Runs	Wkts	Av	Catches
1949	N Zealand	4	158	22	599	16	37.43	0
1950	W Indies	2	47.2	12	121	3	40.33	1
1951	S Africa	2	65	17	168	0	—	0
1952	India	—	—	—	—	—	—	—
1953	Australia	5	143	33	387	8	48.37	3
1954	Pakistan	3	12	4	32	1	32.00	0
1955	S Africa	5	142.5	40	328	9	36.44	1
1956	Australia	4	108.5	39	223	6	37.16	6
1957	W Indies	4	117	37	277	12	23.08	2
1958	N Zealand	4	66	24	93	7	13.28	3
Total		33	860	228	2,228	62	35.93	16

As a batsman: in all Test matches in England

Opps	Mats	Inns	Not out	Runs	HS	Av	100s	50s
Australia	9	12	1	339	71	30.81	0	2
S Africa	7	12	1	293	95	26.63	0	1
W Indies	6	8	2	150	82	25.00	0	1
N Zealand	8	9	3	258	93	43.00	0	2
Pakistan	3	3	1	81	42	40.50	0	0
Total	33	44	8	1,121	—	31.13	0	6

As a bowler: in all Test matches in England

Opps	Mats	Overs	Mdns	Runs	Wkts	Av	Catches
Australia	9	251.5	72	610	14	43.57	9
S Africa	7	207.5	57	496	9	55.11	1
W Indies	6	164.2	49	398	15	26.53	4
N Zealand	8	224	46	692	23	30.08	3
Pakistan	3	12	4	32	1	32.00	0
Total	33	860	228	2,228	62	35.93	17

As a batsman: in Test matches abroad

Opps	Mats	Inns	Not out	Runs	HS	Av	100s	50s
Australia	14	26	3	536	88	23.30	0	3
S Africa	5	10	0	259	80	25.90	0	1
W Indies	5	7	2	193	49	38.60	0	0
N Zealand	4	4	1	181	134	60.33	1	0
Total	28	47	6	1,169	—	28.51	1	4

As a bowler: in Test matches abroad

Opps	Mats	Overs	Mdns	Runs	Wkts	Av	Catches
Australia	14	223.5*	33	763	28	27.25	7
S Africa	5	189.5*	43	232	19	12.21	3
W Indies	5	182	51	459	14	32.78	2
N Zealand	4	88.4	23	174	9	19.33	3
Total	28	413.2 (8b)	76	1,628	70	23.25	15
		270.4 (6b)	74				

*8-ball overs

Appendix 1

As a batsman: career average in all first-class matches

Mats	Inns	Not out	Runs	HS	Av	100s	50s
682	1,072	215	28,641	205	33.42	28	150

Best batting: 205 Essex v Sussex (Eastbourne) 1947

As a bowler: career average in all first-class matches

Mats	Overs	Mdns	Runs	Wkts	Av	Catches
682	18,352.4 (6b) 826.6 (8b)	4,526 (6b) 128 (8b)	48,170	2,082	23.13	427

Best bowling: 10–90 Essex v Lancashire (Clacton) 1949

Appendix 2

Four Scorecards

Oxford v Cambridge at Lord's. July 5, 7, 8 1947
Oxford University

W. G. Keighley (Eton and Trinity) b
Bailey 99

N. C. F. Bloy (Dover and Brasenose) b
Griffiths 9

H. A. Pawson (Winchester and Christ
Church) run out 135

M. P. Donnelly (New Plymouth H.S.,
New Zealand, and Worcester) lbw b
Bailey 81

A. H. Kardar (Punjab Univ. and
University) b Bailey 46

D. F. Henley (Harrow and Trinity) c
Bailey b Mills 52

R. H. Maudsley (Malvern and
Brasenose) b Mills 12

A. W. H. Mallett (Dulwich and
Brasenose) b Mills 10

P. A. Whitcombe (Winchester and
Christ Church) lbw b Mills 6

H. B. Robinson (North Shore College,
Vancouver, and Oriel) b Griffiths 1

W. W. Davidson (Brighton and
Wadham) not out 0

b 5, 1-b 1 6

—

Total   457

Cambridge University

G. L. Willatt (Repton and St Catharine's) c
Pawson b Whitcombe 1   — lbw b Kardar 90

J. Pepper (The Leys and Emmanuel) b
Kardar 13   — c Mallett b Kardar 20

B. G. Cangley (Felsted and Trinity Hall) b
Kardar 23   — b Mallett 38

H. E. Watts (Downside and Peterhouse) c
Mallett b Robinson 65   — c Keighley b Robinson 1

T. E. Bailey (Dulwich and St John's) c
Donnelly b Robinson 9   — not out 60

G. M. Shuttleworth (Queen Elizabeth G.S.,
Blackburn, and King's) c Donnelly b
Robinson 9   — not out 27

D. J. Insole (Monoux School, Walthamstow
and St Catharine's) run out 38   — c Davidson b Robinson 44

P. B. Datta (Asutosh College, Calcutta, and
Trinity Hall) b Robinson 19

N. M. Mischler (St Paul's and St
Catharine's) c Davidson b Kardar 8

J. M. Mills (Oundle and Corpus Christi) b
Kardar 3

W. H. Griffiths (Charterhouse and St
John's) not out 1

B 3, 1-b 8, w 1 12   B 30, 1-b 3, n-b 1 34

—   —

Total   201   Total (5 wkts)   314

Appendix 2

Cambridge University Bowling

	O.	M.	R.	W
Bailey	36	10	112	3
Griffiths	30	7	78	2
Datta	31	6	80	0
Mills	53	11	137	4
Willatt	6	1	20	0
Insole	3	0	24	0

Oxford University Bowling

	O.	M.	R.	W		O.	M.	R.	W
Mallett	27	9	45	0	....	38	21	39	1
Whitcombe	16	5	35	1	....	18	4	31	0
Henley	4	0	8	0					
Kardar	25.3	9	50	4	....	36	19	50	2
Robinson	17	5	51	4	....	30	6	99	2
Pawson						11	3	19	0
Donnelly						6	2	23	0
Bloy						2	0	18	0
Maudsley						2	1	1	0

Umpires: H. G. Baldwin and D. Davies.

England v New Zealand, Second Test at Lord's. June 25, 27, 28 1949

England

J. D. Robertson c Mooney b Cowie	26	— c Cave b Rabone	121
L. Hutton b Burtt	23	— c Cave b Rabone	66
W. J. Edrich c Donnelly b Cowie	9	— c Hadlee b Burtt	31
D. C. S. Compton c Sutcliffe b Burtt	116	— b Burtt	6
A. Watkins c Wallace b Burtt	6	— not out	49
F. G. Mann b Cave	18	— c Donnelly b Rabone	17
T. E. Bailey c Sutcliffe b Rabone	93	— not out	6
T. G. Evans b Burtt	5		
C. Gladwin run out	5		
J. A. Young not out	1		
B 9, l-b 2	11	B 9, l-b 1	10

Total (9 wkts., dec.)	313	Total (5 wkts.)	306

W. E. Hollies did not bat.

New Zealand

B. Sutcliffe c Compton b Gladwin	57	F. L. H. Mooney c Watkins b Young	33
V. J. Scott c Edrich b Compton	42	T. B. Burtt c Edrich b Hollies	23
W. A. Hadlee c Robertson b Hollies	43	H. B. Cave c and b Young	6
W. M. Wallace c Evans b Hollies	2	J. Cowie not out	1
M. P. Donnelly c Hutton b Young	206	B 16, l-b 3, w 3 n-b 1	23
F. B. Smith b Hollies	23		
G. O. Rabone b Hollies	25	Total	484

New Zealand Bowling

	O.	M.	R.	W.		O.	M.	R.	W.
Cowie	26.1	5	64	2	....	14	3	39	0
Cave	27	2	79	1	....	7	1	23	0
Rabone	14	5	56	1	....	28	6	116	3
Burtt	35	7	102	4	....	37	12	58	2
Sutcliffe	1	0	1	0	....	16	1	55	0
Wallace						1	0	5	0

England Bowling

	O.	M.	R.	W.
Bailey	33	3	136	0
Gladwin	28	5	67	1
Edrich	4	0	16	0
Hollies	58	18	133	5
Compton	7	0	33	1
Young	26.4	4	65	3
Watkins	3	1	11	0

FALL OF WICKETS

ENGLAND – First Innings:

1	2	3	4	5	6	7	8	9
48	59	72	83	112	301	307	307	313

ENGLAND – Second Innings:

1	2	3	4	5
143	216	226	226	252

NEW ZEALAND – First Innings:

1	2	3	4	5	6	7	8	9
89	124	137	160	197	273	351	436	464

Umpires: W. H. Ashdown and F. Chester.

Yorkshire v Essex at Leeds. July 23, 25, 26 1960
Essex

G. Barker c Close b Cowan	11	— c Cowan b Close	15
G. J. Smith c Sharpe b Ryan	3	— c D. Wilson b Close	24
†B. Taylor b Ryan	8	— c Sharpe b Close	42
*D. J. Insole c Close b Ryan	17	— c Sharpe b Close	9
T. E. Bailey not out	60	— c Binks b Close	46
M. Bear lbw b Taylor	14	— c Sharpe b D. Wilson	9
B. R. Knight c Sharpe b Taylor	2	— c Birkenshaw b Close	5
W. T. Greensmith b D. Wilson	34	— c Binks b Close	0
L. H. R. Ralph c Stott b D. Wilson	18	— c Binks b Ryan	42
Dr C. B. Clarke b D. Wilson	2	— not out	0
A. Hurd b D. Wilson	0	— c D. Wilson b Close	0
B 9, 1 b 2	11	B 6, n-b 2	8

1/13 2/15 3/23 4/52 5/87 6/93   Total   180
7/151 8/173 9/180 (1.70 an over)

1/41 2/42 3/64 4/99 5/118 Total 200
6/180 7/194 8/195 9/200

Bowling: *First Innings*—Ryan 30—9—64—3; Cowan 24—5—44—1; D. Wilson 13.2—7—13—4; Taylor 19—9—24—2; Close 19—12—24—0; *Second Innings*—Ryan 14—2—42—1; Cowan 17—7—17—0; Taylor 10—4—27—0; Close 23.5—7—43—8; D. Wilson 9—1—37—1; Birkenshaw 3—1—26—0.

Yorkshire

W. B. Stott b Bailey	1	— c Taylor b Knight	6
K. Taylor c Insole b Knight	5	— run out	31
J. B. Bolus lbw b Knight	11	— lbw b Ralph	19
†J. G. Binks b Bailey	4	— c Knight b Bailey	14
D. B. Close b Bailey	24	— c Ralph b Bailey	25
P. J. Sharpe c Knight b Bailey	8	— b Bailey	66
*J. V. Wilson c Taylor b Bailey	3	— c Taylor b Knight	50
J. Birkenshaw not out	13	— b Bailey	0
D. Wilson b Bailey	0	— c Ralph b Bailey	0
M. Ryan b Bailey	15	— c Taylor b Knight	3
M. J. Cowan b Knight	2	— not out	0
		B 13, 1-b 8, w 2	23

1/6 2/8 3/15 4/41 5/45 6/56   Total   86
7/57 8/57 9/77 (1.79 an over)

1/11 2/41 3/84 4/86   Total   237
5/190/6/203 7/203 8/229 9/237

Bowling: *First Innings*—Bailey 24—10—40—7; Knight 15.5—3—36—3; Ralph 8—3—10—0. *Second Innings*—Bailey 33—8—61—5; Knight 24.2—5—59—3; Ralph 15—1—59—1; Clarke 5—1—20—0; Hurd 8—2—15—0.

Umpires: D. Davies and A. E. Rhodes.

Gentlemen v Players at Lord's. July 18, 19, 20, 1962
Gentlemen

Rev. D. S. Sheppard c and b Titmus	112	— b Titmus	34
E. J. Craig b Trueman	4	— c Titmus b Trueman	0
*E. R. Dexter c Trueman b Shackleton	55	— run out	1
M. J. K. Smith run out	44	— not out	15
R. M. Prideaux b Trueman	14	— b Shackleton	109
A. R. Lewis lbw b Shackleton	2	— c Andrew b Titmus	10
R. W. Barber run out	0	— not out	3
D. B. Pithey run out	30		
T. E. Bailey c Walker b Shackleton	5		
†A. C. Smith c Sharpe b Shackleton	33		
O. S. Wheatley not out	14		
B 4, 1-b 6	10		

1/12 2/109 3/204 4/221 5/227 6/229   Total 323
7/239 8/226 9/275

1/0 2/73   Total (5 wkts., dec.) 172
3/95 4/115 5/166

Bowling: *First Innings*—Trueman 13—6—59—2; Shackleton 38—9—101—4; Walker 28—4—64—0; Titmus 20—6—46—1; Gifford 14—4—43—0. *Second Innings*—Shackleton 19—8—38—1; Trueman 10—6—8—1; Titmus 24—5—69—2; Walker 9—2—21—0; Gifford 7—0—36—0.

Players

M. J. Stewart c A. Smith b Bailey	0	— c A. Smith b Wheatley	3
J. H. Edrich b Bailey	19	— not out	77
P. H. Parfitt c Sheppard b Dexter	9	— c Dexter b Barber	63
T. W. Graveney c Craig b Wheatley	21	— c A. Smith b Bailey	41
P. J. Sharpe c and b Barber	39	— not out	12
P. M. Walker b Bailey	15		
F. J. Titmus c Dexter b Bailey	70		
*F. S. Trueman c Wheatley b Barber	63		
†K. V. Andrew c A. Smith b Bailey	17		
N. Gifford c A. Smith b Bailey	2		
D. Shackleton not out	1		
B 4	4	B 1, 1-b 10	88

1/0 2/15 3/41 4/56 5/86 6/104   Total 260
7/194 8/255 9/257

1/3 2/121 3/177   Total (3 wkts.) 207

Bowling: *First Innings*—Bailey 30.3—10—58—6; Wheatley 19—6—37—2; Dexter 18—2—49—1; Barber 21—7—90—2; Pithey 8—2—22—0. *Second Innings*—Bailey 13—1—45—1; Wheatley 12—1—46—1; Pithey 4—0—27—0; Dexter 7—0—35—0; Barber 7—0—43—1.

Umpires: H. Yarnold and A. E. Rhodes.

Index

Adcock, N. A. T., 114–15, 122
Adelaide Oval, 108–9
Allen, Sir George (G.O.), 16, 27, 37, 91, 132, 140
Alleyn Court, 10, 12, 17, 19, 26, 34
Alleyn, Edward, 10
Andrew, K. V., 166
Appleyard, R., 75, 95, 100, 105, 107, 110–11, 113, 116
Archer, Ron, 52, 72, 101
Arlott, John, 1, 158, 160–2
Arsenal FC, 45
Asgarali, N., 124
Ashton, Lt.-Col. Hubert, M. P., 26, 34, 118
Ashton, C. T., 35
Ashton, G., 35
Ashton, Sir H., 35
Aspital, Brian, 166
Attlee, Clement, 20
Avery, A. V., 18, 99

Bailey, Basil, 9–10, 90
Bailey, Greta, 19, 22–3, 91, 108, 124, 162–3, 167
Bailey, Justin, 116
Bailey, Kim, 116
Bailey, Sharon, 124
Bailey, Trevor, the subject of this biography
Bairstow, D. L., 160
Barker, G., 127–8, 152
Barking FC, 46
Barnard, H. M., 128
Barnes, S. F., 24, 53
Barrington, K. F., 117
Bates, D. L., 15
Baxter, Peter, 160–1
Bedford School, 13

Bedser, A. V., 5–6, 25, 32, 38, 43–4, 49, 53–6, 66–7, 69–72, 75, 87, 99, 101, 104–7, 113
Benaud, R., 10, 15, 52, 60–1, 101, 134, 146
Berry, R., 42–3
Botham, I. T., 76, 160
Bourda Cricket Ground, Guyana, 81
Boyce, K. D., 151
Boycott, G., 117
Bradman, Sir Donald, 10, 23–4, 51–2, 151
Brearley, J. M., 160
Brisbane Cricket Ground ('The Gabba'), 43, 102–5, 142
Brown, Bill, 15
Brown, Major C. A., 154
Brown, F. R., 31, 42–4, 54–5, 60, 62–3, 132, 162
Brown, W. A., 24
Burke, Umpire, 84
Bustamente, Alex, 89

Cambridge University, 4, 11, 13, 18–23, 25–6, 32, 35–7, 39, 42, 51, 124, 130
Cannings, V. H. D., 127–8
Cape Town, 120
Cardus, Sir Neville, 65, 157
Carr, D. B., 36
Castor, Brian, 21
Cheetham, J. E., 113
Christ's Hospital, 15
Clark, D. G., 157
Clark, Horace, 47
Close, D. B., 31, 43, 130
Coleman, David, 158
Compton, D. C. S., 14, 30, 43, 45, 52–3, 57–60, 66, 71–2, 75, 82–3, 85, 94–5, 99, 103, 110, 113–14, 119, 122, 158, 168
Condon, Eddie, 111

179

Cook, N. G. B., 41–2
Cotton, Henry, 10
Cowdrey, C. S., 124
Cowdrey, Sir Colin, 75, 99, 101, 103–4, 107, 110, 116, 119, 124, 135–6, 141, 158
Cowdrey, Penny, 124
Cowie, J., 30
Crabtree, H. P., 18, 150
Creek, Norman, 35
Cunis, R. S., 162

Dalton, Harold 'Woozer', 97
Davidson, A.K., 52–3, 56, 60–1, 70, 101, 134, 136
Davies, E. O., 37
de Courcy, J. H., 52
Derbyshire CCC, 154–5
Dewes, J. G., 32, 42–3
Dexter, E. R., 130–1, 137, 141, 149–50
Dimmock, Peter, 158
Doggart, A. G., 35
Doggart, G. H. G., 32, 36
Donnelly, M. P., 22, 29–30
Duckworth, G., 106
Dulwich College, 1, 4, 10–18, 21
Durban, 120–1

Edgbaston, 98, 131, 146, 155
Edrich, J. H., 148
Edrich, W. J., 14, 29, 32, 43, 52, 67, 70, 72, 75, 99, 103–4, 110, 113
Elwes, Polly, 158
Endean, W. R., 121
Essex, CCC, 2, 11, 16, 20–1, 23, 25–9, 31–2, 34, 37, 39–41, 45, 47–9, 82, 89, 91, 96–100, 112, 115–18, 121, 124, 126–8, 130, 141–6, 148–58, 163, 165, 167
Evans, Jean, 108
Evans, R. E., 127
Evans, T. G., 38, 56, 71, 75, 107, 119, 122, 128, 132, 134, 141

Faragher, Harold, 165
Farnes, K., 20
Favell, L. E., 109
Fiddling, K., 37
Fletcher, K. W. R., 144, 150–2
Frindall, Bill, 162

Geary, G., 15
Gee, Harry, 30
Gibson, Alan, 162
Gifford, N., 148
Gilchrist, R., 126
Gillette, Umpire, 84
Glamorgan CCC, 37, 99, 143
Gloucestershire CCC, 18, 91, 131, 155
Goddard, J. D., 38, 126
Goddard, T. L., 113
Graveney, T. W., 53–4, 56–8, 67, 71, 75, 79, 82, 85, 94, 99, 124, 135–6, 158
Gray, J. R., 127–8, 130
Greaves, Jimmy, 158
Green, Geoffrey, 157
Grimmett, Clarrie, 138
Grout, A. T. W., 138
Groves, Vic, 45

Hadlee, W. A., 30
Haileybury, 14
Hagen, Walter, 6
Hammond, W. R., 51
Hampshire CCC, 13, 124, 126–8, 130
Hanif Mohammad, 95
Harvey, Bagenal, 111, 142, 157–8, 163–4
Harvey, R. N., 7, 51, 54, 56, 67, 69, 109, 111
Hassett, A. L., 7, 51–3, 55–6, 58, 61, 63, 66–7, 69, 101
Hastings, Michael Tuke, 162
Hayter, Reg, 80
Headingley, see Leeds
Healey, Denis, 18
Heath, M., 126–8
Heine, P. S., 114–15, 120, 122
Hill, J. C., 52, 55
Hill, Jimmy, 158
Hobbs, Sir Jack, 52, 120
Hobbs, R. N. S., 144, 152
Hole G. B., 52, 58, 67, 69, 71, 109
Hollies, W. E., 29–30, 43
Holmes, E. R. T., 95
Holt, J. K., 81
Horton, H., 128
Howard, Geoffrey, 101
Howard, Nigel, 27
Hutton, Dorothy, 108
Hutton, Sir Leonard, 5, 14, 38, 42, 45, 49, 51,

53–4, 56–9, 65–72, 75–6, 78–80, 82–3, 84–7, 89, 91, 93–6, 99–105, 107–10, 113, 147

Illingworth, R., 141, 143
Ingleby-Mackenzie, A. C. D., 128
Insole, D. J., 21, 25, 32, 36, 39–40, 82, 96–8, 100, 115, 118–21, 123, 127–8, 140, 142, 146
Inzamam Ul-Haq, 42
Iverson, J. B., 45

Jardine, D. R., 75, 104
Jenkins, R. O., 31
Johannesburg (Wanderers ground), 119, 121
Johnson, I. W., 101, 103, 109, 116
Johnston, Brian, 160, 162
Johnston, W. A., 52, 58, 60–1, 70–1

Kanhai, R. B., 126
Kensington Oval, 81
Kent CCC, 13–14, 16, 44, 114, 150
Kentish, E. S. M., 81
Kenyon, D., 53, 56, 58
Kiddle, Horace, 1, 14
King, F. McD., 89
King, I. M., 128
Kline, L. F., 135
Knight, B. R., 144, 149, 151–2, 156

Laker, J. C., 31, 43, 65–7, 69, 72, 75, 82, 99, 101, 114, 116–17, 131–3, 137, 149–51
Lancashire CCC, 3, 31–2, 34, 42
Langley, G. R. A., 55, 58, 70, 109
Langridge, James, 41
Leeds (Headingley), 29, 65, 69, 114, 116, 126, 131, 143, 146
Leicestershire CCC, 51, 156
Lemmon, David, 25
Leveson-Gower, Sir Henry, 147
Leystonstone FC, 27, 34, 36, 45
Lindwall, R. R., 6, 28, 32, 44, 51–3, 56–8, 60–3, 66, 70–1, 102, 104, 106, 109–10, 137–9
Loader, P. J., 75, 118, 133–4
Lock, G. A. R., 31, 66–7, 69, 71–2, 75, 79, 82, 101, 114, 116–17, 123, 131, 133–4, 137
Longford, Lord, 162
Lord's 5, 7, 15–16, 21, 27, 29, 38, 40, 42, 50, 54–7, 59–60, 62, 65, 69, 75, 79, 93, 95, 116, 124, 126, 131, 142, 146–8

Maddocks, L. V., 107, 109

Malan, Basil, 121
Mallett, A. W. H., 14, 21
Manchester (Old Trafford), 31, 38, 65–6, 114, 117
Manchester United FC, 47
Mann, F. G., 162
Mann, Tufty, 162
Marriott, C. S., 14–15
Marshall, Mike, 25
McConnon, J. E., 99
McDonald, C. C., 52
McGlew, D. J., 113, 123
McLean, R. A., 113, 115
McWatt, C. A., 84
Marlar, RG, 148
Marshall, R. E., 127–8
Martin-Jenkins, Christopher, 160
May, P.B.H., 22, 53–4, 70–1, 75, 81–2, 85, 95, 99, 101, 103–4, 107–8, 110, 113, 116, 119, 122, 124, 132, 134, 136–7, 141–2
Meckiff, I., 134–7
Melbourne (MCG), 7, 43, 105–7, 136, 138–9
Menzies, Umpire, 84
Middlesex CCC, 13, 16, 43, 91, 95
Miller, K. R., 6, 23, 28, 32, 44, 51–3, 56–8, 60–2, 66, 69, 70–1, 101, 110–11, 116, 139
Milton, C. A., 141
Montgomery, S., 37
Morris, A. R., 51–3, 55, 57, 67, 70, 102
Mortimore, John, 131

Noble, Alf, 34
Northamptonshire CCC, 37, 41, 100
Nottingham (Trent Bridge), 40, 48, 53–5, 94–5, 116, 124, 141
Nottinghamshire CCC, 31, 96, 115, 154
Nutter, A. E., 37

Oakman, A. S. M., 119
Old Trafford, *see* Manchester
O'Neill, N. C., 136
Oval, Kennington, 42, 68–70, 113–14, 160
Oxford University, 14, 20, 22, 35–6, 51

Palmer, C. H., 78
Parker, Grahame, 18
Parkhouse, W. G. A., 43
Parkinson, Michael, 164
Parks, J. M., 143
Paterson, R. F. T., 26, 47

Pawson, H. A., 36
Pearce, T. N., 23–4, 32, 39, 153
Perks, R. T. D., 40
Perth (WACA), 102, 105
Port Elizabeth, 122
Port-of-Spain, Trinidad, 84–5

Queen's Park Oval, 81

Rabone, G. O., 30
Rae, A. F., 40
Ramadhin, S., 37–8, 40, 81–2, 124
Rhodes, A. E. G., 148
Richardson, P. E., 116, 118, 120, 122, 124, 136
Ring, D. T., 15, 52, 55, 58–63
Rist, F. H., 24, 144
Robertson, J. D., 13, 43
Robins, R. W. V., 95
Rorke, G. F., 137
Ross, Alan, 107, 111, 162
Rostron, Frank, 59
Rumsey, F. E., 162
Russell, Jack, 56

Sabina Park (Kingston, Jamaica), 81, 86
Salim Malik, 42
Shackleton, D., 127–8
Sheppard, Rt. Rev. D. S., 42–3, 91, 94–6
Shirreff, A. C., 13
Simpson, R. T., 31, 53–4, 66, 95, 99, 104
Smith, O. G., 126
Smith, G., 16
Smith, P. A., 39
Smith, Ray, 18, 23–5, 39, 49, 115
Sobers, Sir Garfield, 126, 158, 166
Somerset CCC, 13, 155
Southend United FC, 2, 34
Statham, J. B., 5, 48, 54, 65, 69, 75, 81–2,
    84–7, 89, 95, 99–101, 104, 106–8, 110–11,
    114, 118, 120, 124, 126, 137, 141
Stewart, M. J., 148
Stockport County FC, 47
Stollmeyer, J. B., 81
Subba Row, R., 132, 134
Surrey CCC, 16, 51, 95, 148
Sussex CCC, 41, 78, 143, 148, 150
Sutcliffe, H., 29, 52, 120
Sutcliffe, W. H. H., 140, 147
Suttle, K. G., 78
Swanton, E. W., 59, 83, 162

Sydney (SCG), 44, 104, 106, 110, 137
Tallon, D., 54
Tattersall, R., 54–5
Tavare, C. J., 161
Tayfield, H. J., 113, 121
Taylor, B., 118, 126–8, 153, 156
Taylor, Reg, 124
Titmus, F. J., 143
Trent Bridge, *see* Nottingham
Trueman, F. S., 1, 5, 7, 69, 71, 75, 78–9, 87,
    117, 124, 131, 137, 140–1, 147, 161
Tyson, F. H., 5, 75, 99–101, 104–8, 110–11,
    114, 118, 120, 122, 130, 134, 158

Valentine, A. L., 37–8, 40, 81–2, 124
van der Bijl, P. G., 162
van Ryneveld, C. B., 120–1
Vengsarkar, D. G., 160
Vigar, F. H., 24, 98

Wade, T. H., 39
Walker, P. M., 143
Wallace, M. W., 29
Walcott, C. L., 37, 81, 85, 126
Walcott, Umpire, 42
Walthamstow Avenue FC, 5, 45–7, 98
Wardle, J. H., 53, 56, 63, 75, 105, 107, 120
Warner, Sir Pelham, 16
Warr, J. J., 42–4
Warwickshire CCC, 29, 145–6, 149, 155
Washbrook, C., 14
Wasim Akram, 41
Watson, W., 5, 50, 54, 58–62, 65–6, 82, 84–5,
    99, 132, 134, 136–7
Weekes, E. D., 37, 41, 81, 85, 126
Wight, Peter, 42
Wilcox, Denys, 5, 10–12, 19, 21
Wilcox, John, 11
Willis, R. G. D., 160–1
Wilson, J. V., 99
Winslow, P. L., 113
Woodcock, John, 3, 6, 50, 103
Wooller, W., 140
Worcestershire CCC, 40, 52, 145
Worrell, Sir Frank, 37, 41, 81, 84–5, 126
Wright, D. V. P., 43–4

Yardley, N. W. D., 38, 162
Yorkshire CCC, 50–2, 78, 91, 95, 99, 130,
    143, 148